52 WAYS TO MAKE FAMILY TRAVEL MORE ENJOYABLE

Kate Redd

OLIVER
NELSON

THOMAS NELSON PUBLISHERS
Nashville

To
Mom and Dad,
who taught me the
fun of traveling

and

Craig Stuart, Twila Jean,
Roberta June, Janice Leigh,
Carl Frederick, Beverly Grace,
Jeffrey Craig, and Christi Rena—
my fellow adventurers
through the years

Copyright © 1994 by Jan L. Dargatz

Published in Nashville, Tennessee, by Thomas Nelson, Inc., Publishers, and distributed in Canada by Word Communications, Ltd., Richmond, British Columbia.

Library of Congress Cataloging-in-Publication Data
Redd, Kate.
    52 ways to make family travel more enjoyable / Kate Redd.
        p.   cm.
    ISBN 0-8407-9212-3 (pbk.)
    1. Travel. 2. Family recreation. I. Title. II. Title: Fifty-two ways to make family travel more enjoyable.
G151.R43   1994
910′.2′02—dc20   93-48446
                                                                        CIP

Printed in the United States of America.

1   2   3   4   5   6   —   99   98   97   96   95   94

Contents

Travel Activities Along the Way

Making the Trip Easier for Everyone

It's Your Child's Vacation, Too!

🚗 Introduction

Making the Vacation Fun

I n this book you'll find simple and practical tips to make family travel more enjoyable. The operative word to remember always is *fun*.

Vacations are meant to be fun. Ask yourself as you plan a trip:

- What do I like to do for fun?

- What does my spouse like to do for fun?

- What does my child like to do for fun?

- What did I like to do for fun when I was a child?

Think back to vacations that you really enjoyed as a child. If you never had a vacation that was truly fun for you, imagine what you would have liked as a child.

Vacations truly are for the young at heart—regardless of age. Your family vacation should be a time when you all have fun and you can all be like children on an adventure together.

Make having fun the foremost goal of your trip as a family. Keep it as your mind-set, your perspective, your number one item on the agenda. When an event or activity ceases to be fun, move on to the next one.

As best you can, accommodate and plan for things that are fun for each person. That may take some compromise, but it's doable.

Fun is usually the description we use for events, activities, and experiences that

- make us laugh.

- make us feel valued or special in some way.

- cause us to see life, others, or the world around us in a new way.

- rest pleasantly in our memories.

Fun is very difficult to have when one is tired, in a grumpy mood, in a cramped space, or when one is being given directions and admonitions at every turn.

Many adults think of a vacation as a time to relax. How many parents have said to their children about an upcoming vacation, "We're going to relax and have fun together"? Children, however, tend to think of a vacation as a time of exploration and of high energy output. The two perspectives are like oil and water. If you want to relax as an adult, go away with other adults who also want to relax. Or find a resort that can satisfy your desire to relax and your child's desire to play. Otherwise, expect your family vacation to sap your strength physically.

Communication, camaraderie, and closeness mix with having fun. Use your vacation as a time for talking with your child and for having shared experiences.

Above all, engage in the process of being together. Focus on being with your family. Keep your mind on the concerns and uniqueness of those with whom you are traveling, not on the work and responsibilities you left behind.

A giant step toward making a family vacation more enjoyable is desiring that it be enjoyable for each person. Choose to have a good time together. And then find ways to enhance that decision. Here are 52 suggestions.

1 🚗 Child-Friendly Places

As you plan your destination or itinerary, keep this idea at the forefront of your thinking: *child friendly*.

If you are planning a cruise, think about the Big Red Boat (Disney's cruise ship for families) gliding through the waters off the coast of Florida rather than the mostly-retired-folks cruise that's ideal for gazing at glaciers in Alaska.

If you are planning a trip to the mountains, think about a family campground that has plenty of well-marked trails and other amenities, such as a pool or fishing pier, rather than a cabin isolated from contact with the outside world.

If you are going to the beach, think about a Club Med family resort with plenty of activities for children rather than a honeymooners' delight.

You don't need to spend a lot of money in choosing a child-friendly place. Quite the opposite! Family resorts, motels and hotels that welcome families, and campgrounds are usually less expensive than their adult-only counterparts. At the same time, you don't need to limit yourself to fast-food outlets or really low-budget motels.

Restaurants and Hotels In choosing places to eat and to sleep, seek out places that

- allow for and expect guests to be in casual attire.

- have children's menus.

- have playgrounds, pools, or other features designed especially for use by children.

- are amenable to noise.

- have been designed with child safety in mind.

- openly welcome children!

How can you tell if a place welcomes children? Look for the advertising that says so. Watch for signs or descriptions that include the words *family, children, play,* and *fun.* Look for bright colors, easy-to-clean surfaces and fabrics, and open spaces. Such a place has usually planned for children.

There's nothing more uncomfortable for you or your child than to find yourself in a place where your child can't move or can't laugh out loud. Such a place just isn't any fun.

Entertainment and Supervision As you evaluate a destination point for your family vacation, be on the alert for those who can help you create safe and creative fun for your child. Are playgrounds or pools supervised by qualified adults? Are play areas well maintained? Are they free of debris and fenced? Is play equipment sturdy and in good repair? Is the entertainment geared toward the child's level of understanding?

Does the resort or camp provide children's activities that are properly supervised and designed to be age appropriate for a wide spectrum of ages? Is a baby-sitting service provided for evening hours? Are medical facilities and personnel readily accessible?

Many hotels make adult video programming readily available on their in-house television systems. You'll probably want to make provisions to block off those channels from your child's viewing.

2 🚗 Stay on a Schedule

Every family has something of a daily eating-and-sleeping schedule for nonvacation days. Unfortunately, families on vacation frequently throw those schedules to the wind when they leave home. The result is too often cranky, crabby, irritable, and short-tempered children and parents.

Bedtime Stay in your normal routine as much as possible. Don't expect a child who is accustomed to a 7:00 A.M. to 9:00 P.M. day to adjust readily to a 5:30 A.M. to 11:00 P.M. schedule.

Unwinding Time Vacation days are sometimes filled with so many new and unusual sights, sounds, and experiences that a little one becomes overly stimulated and has difficulty going to sleep right away. Allow for decompression from the day's events. Take a slow evening stroll. Curl up with your child and a good book you can read aloud. Play soft music. Dim the lights. Settle into your room and into the mood for rest.

Nap Time If your young child normally takes a nap, provide for that while you're on vacation, too.

Nap time may be a good time for driving from one destination to the next. If you're at a park or resort, designate a quiet time and place for your young child to rest. If you are at an amusement park, you may want to take a couple of hours out of the day and return to your motel or hotel room for a nap.

Mealtimes Plan to eat at times you normally eat at home. Stop at a restaurant or picnic site a half hour in advance of your normal mealtime in order to keep your schedule. Allow for the time it takes to use a rest room and wash hands, be seated, order, and have the food prepared. Also provide snacks on schedule.

Plenty of Fluids Remember that you are all likely to be exerting more energy than usual on a vacation, and since most family vacations are scheduled during summer months, you and your child will be especially prone to dehydration. Keep the liquids flowing. Stop frequently at drinking fountains. If you are traveling by car, you may want to have a canteen or plastic bottle of water for each person. (Start the day with the containers full of ice and add water as needed.)

Avoid getting overly tired, overly thirsty, or overly hungry. You'll all have more fun.

3 🚗 Child-Made Decisions

Let your child assist in the decisions that are made both before and during a vacation. Not only will this be fun for your child, but your child will be more satisfied with each day's activities.

Reasonable Choices Set out parameters and boundaries prior to decision making. Let your child know limits related to

- time: "We will have only two hours to look at the shops today."

- expense: "You need to choose something from the menu that will be a total of four dollars or under."

- space constraints: "Try to locate a room that has two double beds."

Give your child multiple-choice or either-or options: "You can either go swimming after we get back to the motel or spend a half hour playing on the play equipment here at the restaurant. Which would you rather do?"

Trade-Offs In many ways, your child's ability to make decisions related to a vacation is unlike his decision-making opportunities in his normal routine. Your child is likely to have very few chances on a family vacation to say where he wants to go next—unlike unrestricted movement around your home. On a normal summer day, your child can probably choose what he wants to wear. He may not have that privilege each day of your vacation. On the other hand, your child will probably have a lot more leeway in deciding what he wants to eat. Discuss these trade-offs with your child, and point out ways in which he is privileged on vacation to make some decisions he doesn't normally get to make.

Destination Decisions Discuss your family vacation with your child as soon as you begin to plan it. Talk about places to visit and experiences to have. Daydream together. And then help your child learn how to turn dreams into concrete plans, including the realities of budgets and time limitations.

Be conservative in estimating how many days it may take to get to and from a destination. Discuss various modes of travel with your child: "We can afford to fly and have three days there, or drive and have four days there. If we drive, we'll have two long days in the car each way. Which sounds more fun to you?"

Discuss areas you might like to explore: "Would you rather camp out this year or go to the beach?"

Or you might offer, "If we went to the city, here are several things we might do. Which of those activities sounds fun to you?"

If your child has never been to the beach, the forest, or the big city, she'll probably not be able to make informed choices. Talk to your child in terms she can understand: "If we go to the beach, we'll probably spend only about two or three hours each day on the beach. You'd be able to make sand castles, collect shells, and get in the surf. You'd swim, however, in the pool at the motel. The rest of the time we'll be eating, exploring some of the shops in the town, or resting in our room." A vacation at the beach may sound to your child as if she's going to be on the beach from dawn to dusk. Better to discuss expectations in advance of the trip than midway through the vacation.

Route Mapping   Get out a map as you plan your itinerary. Let your child help make decisions about which routes to take. Highways are great for making good time over long distances, but back roads and scenic routes are nearly always more interesting.

Daily Choices   Permit your child to have a say in where you eat and where you spend the night. Not only will your child feel a little more involved in the trip, he'll gain valuable skills in how to travel. Let your child provide input on where you stop for lunch—again, given boundaries. Take along booklets for various motel or hotel chains (most of which are free and can be requested in advance of your trip by calling toll-free numbers), and let your child help scout out suitable-sounding places.

Alternate Choices   Encourage your child to prioritize choices and have a Plan B. Let your child know in advance that you have veto power over any decision. At the same time, be open to some of the possibilities your child may suggest.

Taking Turns   If you have more than one child, you may want to designate certain choices to various members of your family on a daily basis. For example, let one child designate who sleeps where on one day, and another child the next. Or let one child choose your lunch stop one day, and another child the next.

4 🚗 A Personal Travel Bag

Have a personal travel bag for your child. The bag should be small and light enough so that the child can carry it. Your child should be responsible for the whereabouts of the bag and for its contents. This personal bag should be considered confidential.

The bag might be used for

- souvenirs and memorabilia gathered during the trip—everything from rocks and shells to brochures and extra postcards.

- personal allotments of snacks, gum, or money that may be dispensed by parents along the way.

- small toys, books, and games that the child chooses to take from home.

- any other small personal items—such as sunglasses or hair barrettes.

The bag itself might be a plastic shopping bag with a drawstring top or perhaps the backpack your child normally takes to school. The bag should be sturdy and capable of being closed to keep contents from spilling out.

Pack It Early Ask your child to gather together the items he wants to take in his personal bag at least a day before the trip, and then have him carry it around a bit. He should be able to carry the bag easily for a couple of hundred yards without tiring. In other words, he should be able to carry it into the airport and onto the plane by himself!

Activities En Route A child's personal bag is the place for her to store any games or toys she might want to play with while in the car or on a plane, ship, or train. Suggest that she take things with lots of play hours built into them, such as

- an activity book or puzzle book.

- a small game—a hand-held computer, chess, or checkers game (especially games with pegs or magnets).

- an art kit—a pad of blank paper, a coloring book and crayons, a notebook and pencils.

- a small piece of handwork.

- a self-contained single-person game or puzzle.

- a small toy—a small doll, stuffed animal, or miniature diecast car.

- several books to read.

Basics   Consider outfitting your child with

- a camera—an inexpensive automatic variety is fine. A child should feel free to take pictures within a specified number of rolls of film.

- a map, so your child can follow along on the itinerary you've chosen.

- stationery supplies—a plastic bag with a pen, a pencil, crayons, stickers, postcard postage stamps, and various other age-appropriate writing or art tools.

- an address book for reference when sending cards to friends.

- a trip journal book for recording special memories.

- a coin purse for keeping personal money in one place.

You can put such a bag together for twenty dollars or less and provide hours of travel fun for your child.

5 🚗 The Limited Day

Don't try to cram too much into one day.

Keep in mind that from your child's perspective, one special event in a day can be a wonderful treat!

Cherish Small-Scale Moments The special activity or event doesn't need to be something expensive or tremendously unusual. In our family's history, each of these was considered a very special treat:

- Swimming in a motel pool (especially since we didn't have a pool at home)

- Staying up until 9:30 (an hour past bedtime) to watch a video in a hotel room

- Being allowed to play on the playground equipment in a park across from the motel for an entire hour

- Playing video games at an arcade for half an hour

- Taking an early morning hike around the lake before leaving for a full day of driving

- Stopping to watch the bears feed in a dump site in a national park

- Riding the inexpensive trolley car around "old town" after supper

- Getting to ride the glass elevator four times in a row—all the way to the top and bottom —before finally getting off on our floor

- Stopping by the side of the road to watch the elk graze in a meadow

See the World Through Your Child's Eyes   As you travel, try to see the world through your child's eyes. What pricks her interest? About what does she get excited? What sparks her creativity?

Think to yourself, *If I was his age, I'd really want to . . . ,* and then make that wish come true for your child even before you're asked.

For a child, a big day can be

- doing something your child doesn't normally get to do, such as walking all the way to the end of the pier and back.

- learning something new, perhaps learning to read a compass.

- trying something he's never tried before, such as going down a water slide.

- having a new experience, such as cycling the paddle boats in the city park.

6 🚗 The Limited Vacation

Don't spend too many days away.

A good rule of thumb is to spend one day away for the average age of your children (or in the case of one child, the age of your child). In other words, for a family with children who are four and six years old, plan a five-day vacation. A family with children ages two, seven, and nine might take a six-day vacation. (The nine-year-old will make it easily; the two-year-old will probably find that length of trip a stretch.)

When Flying Count your travel days as full days. They will be to your child! The flight will hold lots of activity and excitement for your child or young teen. Give yourself plenty of time to adjust to new time zones.

When Driving Don't try to travel too many miles in one day. Count the hours that you really want to be cooped up in the car together on any given day, and multiply by fifty. Don't plan to cover more miles than that in a day.

For example, if you think you can handle two hours in the car in the morning and three hours in the car in the afternoon, plan to cover about 250 miles maximum. Take a look at your map and see about where you'd end the day's journey. Don't stray from that destination more than 50 miles, which would be an extra hour. Keep in mind that for every two hours you drive, you'll probably spend at least one hour in stops for gasoline, rest room breaks, refreshments, meals, and souvenir purchases. Be sure to budget in time you may want to spend at a tourist attraction, special event, or general sightseeing.

Once There Upon arrival at your destination point, give yourselves a little time to rest, unpack, and plan before hurling yourselves into activity. Take a little time to explore your hotel, motel, or resort. Get a feel for where things are located and what facilities and services are available.

Try to arrive at your destination during daylight hours so you can find your way more easily and get settled in before dinner and any evening activities or events. You and your child will feel more at home in a strange place and have a greater sense of security.

Highlights Choose your trip highlights carefully. Having one or two major moments for every three days is a good rule of thumb when touring. A major moment might be

- an amusement park.
- a national park or forest, or a state beach.

- a major city attraction.

- a museum or gallery geared especially for children.

- a hall of fame or themed exhibit.

- a special event, such as a major league game, a play, a concert, or a planetarium show.

When traveling to a major resort or amusement attraction, such as Disney World and Epcot Center, plan to spend more than one day exploring all the park has to offer. The same holds for prominent national parks, such as Yosemite or Yellowstone. Your family can easily spend four or five days in such a place and find something new to do each day.

7 🚗 Stay Within Your Budget

Limits Set a spending limit for each day of your trip. Factor in the special costs that might occur on a certain day, such as the day you visit Sea World or the afternoon you take in a matinee on Broadway. If you exceed your limit one day, tighten the reins on your pocketbook the next. Record all of your expenses for a day. Work out day-to-day averages. Keep running totals so you know where you are in your spending on a daily basis. Let your children do the math for you. They may not understand all that it took for you to earn the money you are spending or the relative cost of items, but they can understand subtraction!

Encourage your children to come up with suggestions on how to save money. Again, offer them decision-making options: "Would you rather have a hamburger for lunch and see a movie tonight, or go to the zoo now and have a picnic there?"

Bargains Also let your children scout out bargains for you. Children are especially good at scouting out the lowest gasoline prices, and your teens may consider it a personal challenge to find the lowest possible air fares. Your older children may find bargain hunting a real challenge. Think of bargains in terms of a financial safari. Make the challenge fun: "How much vacation *can* we get for these dollars?"

Funds Management Here are five more very practical suggestions about managing your trip funds:

1. *Never promise your children that you are going to do something—visit a particular place or take in a certain attraction—and then pull that promise* If you have a doubt about whether you'll be able to afford a particular event, don't bring it up as a possibility. If you find later that you can afford it, make it a surprise! You'll double the enjoyment level for those things you can do and avoid disappointment about those things you can't do.

2. *Give your children spending limits at mealtimes* As with the first suggestion, a few words ahead of time—"Tonight we'll skip the desserts"—can avoid disappointment or unhappy scenes later.

3. *Meter out souvenir or miscellaneous money to each child on a daily basis* Let each child pay for snacks, postcards, and memorabilia from that fund. When the child's money is spent, don't dig into your pockets to advance more. Your child will learn a little about cash flow management during the trip and have only herself to blame for lack of

funds when that "perfect something" makes its appearance.

You may want to set aside an amount of money for each child to spend on a major souvenir. Keep that money in your wallet. Let your child have fun comparison shopping for just the right thing to take back home.

4. *Use traveler's checks* Keep your spending on credit cards to a bare minimum; it's too easy to overspend your daily budget. Avoid carrying too much cash; it's too easy to lose it.

If you are traveling with teenagers, you may want to give them a few traveler's checks of their own. This will keep you from being asked at every turn, "Can I have this?" or from feeling guilty that you aren't buying a major item for your teen at each stop. Let each teen do the choosing and the spending. You may want to match (in some proportion) the amount of money your older child or teen saves for the vacation, giving an added incentive to planning ahead for the trip.

5. *Budget in a contingency for unexpected expenses* You may have underestimated the cost of a particular item (fuel, lodging, meals), or you may encounter emergencies along the way (such as a visit to a local clinic or a problem with your automobile). Set aside a designated amount in your vacation budget for such contingencies. If you don't need to spend it, you can always have one final fling on your last night of the trip!

8 🚗 Phone Home Periodically

Phone home every few days. It's far better to check on things than to worry about them.

Check in with your house sitter every day or so.

Clear your answering machine every few days.

You may want to call a neighbor to make certain that everything seems normal at your house and in your yard. (Are the newspapers being delivered even though you requested that they be stopped? Have circulars been left on your porch that need to be removed? Is the house sitter or yard keeper doing all that you paid him in advance to do?)

The Office Call If you must for your own sense of well-being and emotional rest, phone your office periodically. Let your associates know in advance of your vacation that you'll be phoning but that you want to deal only with emergencies or crises. Keep in mind that most situations can be resolved by others on-site. You may want to make your calls to your office early in the morning so you have the rest of the day either to deal with a situation or to proceed worry free.

Pet Care   If you have placed your animal in the care of a friend or veterinarian, call to check on your animal's well-being. If there's a problem, do what you can to authorize required care or treatment for the animal until you return.

Friends   Let your child phone a friend at least once on the trip. The child will feel more in touch with what is happening at home and be less homesick. (Yes, it is possible to get homesick even when you are traveling with your beloved family!) Your teenager, especially, is likely to enjoy the trip more if he can stay in touch with friends back home periodically. As one teenager said on a family vacation, "I can handle the scary rides at the amusement park. I just can't handle the suspense about what might be happening at home!"

"We Survived!"   Call those who may be concerned about your safety if you encounter a situation that involves any type of danger, delay, or natural disaster. Let your relatives and friends back home know that you are alive and well.

If you change your itinerary, let relatives and friends know that, too. Even on vacation, you'll want others to be able to reach you in an emergency.

A three-minute call is a cheap price to pay for peace of mind or the opportunity to rectify a troublesome situation before it reaches major proportions.

9 🚗 Something for Everyone

As you plan your trip in advance, include something that will be a special treat for each person in your family. If your teenage son, Billy, is a car enthusiast, stop by the Speedway in Indianapolis, and label the event "Billy's special treat." Or take a couple of hours one evening while you are away from home to go with Billy to a showroom to get a close-up look at his favorite vehicle make and model. You might even test-drive one together.

Granted, others in your family may enjoy the tour at the Indianapolis 500 Speedway or the visit to the showroom, but let everyone in your family know that "this one's for Billy."

When you get to Minneapolis, treat your shopaholic teenage daughter, Laura, to an afternoon at Mall America. The rest of your family members will enjoy Camp Snoopy, the Legos store, and various other features of the mall, but call this "Laura's special event."

If each person has a special event scheduled during your family vacation, family members are more likely to be patient and understanding during another family member's special treat.

Special treats allow each person to feel special

and to do something personally enjoyable. Other family members learn a little more about compromise, respect, and activities or events they wouldn't normally seek out on their own.

Daily Treats   What you have planned as part of the whole of your vacation, also plan for each day. Let one moment, event, or treat be special for each member of your family. It may be an extra half hour of sleep for Mom while Dad takes the children to McDonald's for breakfast (and brings back a breakfast burrito for Mom). It may be an ice-cream cone at the end of the day with each child allowed to choose a favorite flavor. It may be a half hour by the stream for Dad and Junior to throw a hook into the water while Mom cleans up from the picnic and the baby takes a nap. It may be allowing your teenager to roam at will through the botanical gardens while you rest your weary feet by the lily pond.

Divide and Conquer   Not every family member needs to experience every moment that all other family members experience. Dad and daughter may want to ride the trolley cars while Mom and son shop in San Francisco. Dad and the children might want to go deep-sea fishing while Mom spends her morning exploring the local galleries in the beach town.

10 🚗 Keep Expectations Low

Don't overstate in advance the fun you expect to have as a family. Avoid making comments such as,

- "This will be the greatest family vacation ever."

- "You won't believe how much fun this is going to be."

- "This is going to be the trip of a lifetime."

It may not be.

Choose, instead, to understate and downplay expectations. That way, if the event or experience is less than desirable, you haven't built up your child for a disappointment. On the other hand, if the experience turns out to be a stellar one, you'll all have the benefit of a pleasant surprise!

Make statements such as the following:

- "Let's see what we can see."

- "Let's discover what this is like."

- "Let's explore."

• "Let's try this. Who knows? We might like it!"

Such statements foster a spirit of adventure and experimentation. They build on a child's curiosity.

The Unfun Event   If an event turns out to be a disaster—a truly lousy performance, an incredibly boring pace, a very cheap imitation—find something about it to enjoy. Laugh about what you've just seen or tried. You might label it the dud of the trip. On one family vacation, we kept a running tally of weirdest moments and most strange encounters. If we experienced a disappointment, it made our list with a laugh!

Even the dullest, most outlandish, or huge-flop event can become a choice moment for family laughter. Sometimes the dud event becomes the prime vacation memory if for no other reason than it brought the family into agreement about how terrible an experience it was.

Time Limitations   Let your child know in advance how much time you expect to spend at the event that turns out to be a raving success. "One more ride," "one more hour," or "one more turn" can wear a parent out, even as patience is wearing thin. If you are going to spend only two hours at the fun place, let your child know that in advance. While you might be flexible from time to time, let your child know that an extension of fun time is a rare happening, not the norm. Don't heed pleading. If you do, you'll hear an increasing amount of it in days ahead.

Many a parent has been heard to say, "We'll see how tired you are when that time comes and make a decision then," or "Just look at you. You can hardly hold your eyes open, and you still want to stay longer?" The child who is challenged about his degree of tiredness will do his best to prove to a parent that he has plenty of energy left—all the way back to the motel! Don't fall into that trap. You don't need a reason for calling an end to a fun day or a fun experience, or for setting realistic time limitations.

11 🚗 Choose Activity Over Passivity

A child needs activity. A child is a creature who prefers motion. Being strapped into a car or airline seat is not a child's idea of freedom.

Action! As much as you can, build action into your family vacation. You don't necessarily need to be active in order for your child to be. You can sit quietly in the shade or on the park bench or stop to sip a soda in the cabana. But let your child

- splash his way through the water park to his heart's content.

- go down the slide and climb on the jungle gym five dozen times.

- jump on the giant balloon trampoline at the burger stand for fifteen minutes (before she eats).

- run all the way down to the end of the path —or to the pilings on the beach or to the end of the block—and back.

When you stop for gasoline or rest room stops, let your child do a series of exercises. Simple Simon just might say a dozen jumping jacks, five bend-overs, and ten squat thrusts! One family took along a jump rope for each child and used the fifteen-minute gasoline stops as jumping opportunities.

Rather than spend your lunchtimes in a restaurant, try take-out food and get directions to the local park. Let your child play with the ball or Frisbee you have brought along before or after you eat.

Encourage your child to take full advantage of a motel swimming pool or the opportunity to skip along the riverside path. But don't compromise on safety. You or your spouse should accompany your child at all times.

Advantages   The more energy your child exerts along the way,

- the more willing your child will be to sit quietly in the car and enjoy the passing views.

- the better your child will sleep at night and the more quickly she will wind down at the end of the day.

- the healthier your child will stay on the trip (the active child usually experiences fewer digestive and bowel problems).

- the happier your child will be about the entire vacationing experience!

12 🚗 Advance a Sense of Adventure

Always be on the lookout for the new and the unusual opportunity to explore and to learn. Parents need to realize that learning and exploring are fun for a child. In fact, few things are as exciting to a child as trying something for the first time, learning something new, or making a discovery.

A truly enjoyable family vacation is usually marked by these qualities:

- Wonderment at what has just been seen or experienced

- Wondering what lies around the next bend

- Wandering—freedom to explore an area (whether a park, city, or state) without a map, timetable, or agenda

Getting into the Process Many adults are task oriented when it comes to their family vacations. They plan a trip the way they would plan a project at work: things to do, timetables to keep, and lists to check off.

A child, on the other hand, is much more process oriented. A child takes far more delight in doing an activity than in accomplishing it, mastering it, or relishing in its completion.

Relax and go with the flow of your child. If you are able to engage in the process, without an eye toward task completion, you'll have a lot more fun, and so will the rest of your family!

The Right Questions   Rather than ask *who, where, when,* or *what* questions about your vacation, ask *how* and *why.* The former are questions that result in task completion and delegation of chores. The latter are questions that promote creativity, curiosity, and a sense of adventure.

Pretend   Your child—all the way through teen years—can probably be coaxed into a game of pretend. Let your child make up some of the scenarios as you travel. In the case of a young child, you'll probably need to prime the pump:

- "Pretend you own this city. What parts of it would you change? Where would you live? What kind of life do you think you'd have?"

- "Let's pretend we don't speak the language of the people who live in this part of the country. How would we get around? What would we do to survive?"

13 🚗 Debrief the Experience

Talk over an event or experience with your child. He'll have greater insights into the value of what he has just seen or done, and he'll be able to recall the experience more vividly at a later time.

Talk About It After you've left a place, talk about what you did there. Ask all sorts of questions.

Descriptive questions Ask, "What did you see? What did you do? Where did you go? Who did what?"

Evaluative questions Ask, "What part of this place (or experience or event) did you like best? What would you like to see the next time you visit here? What in this place would you like to show your children someday? If you could change anything about this place (or event), what would you change and why?"

Don't ask, "Did you like that?" Leave yourself some room for a conversation. If a child is negative about an event or experience, explore why she had an adverse reaction.

Imaginative questions Ask your child to extend the experience into the realm of the creative: "Would you like to live in a place like that? What would it be like? Why would you like it? What about it wouldn't you like? What would you work hard to change? What would you like to see stay the same? What do you suppose it's like to work in that place (or perform in that event)?"

Keep "Best of" Lists As you travel, start some lists, such as the following:

- First-time experiences

- New places visited

- Unusual sights and sounds

- Best meals

- Favorite moments

You might want to develop a rating system for certain events and experiences: "That was a five star!" or "That was definitely the best so far!" or "That was a nine plus."

Consult your running logs periodically and recall certain moments. Your child is likely to be in such eager anticipation of the next event or place that he will lose sight of where he's been. Help him to remember what he's done, seen, and felt.

14 🚗 Use Conflicts as Opportunities

Nothing goes 100 percent according to plans—even the most carefully mapped-out ones! Furthermore, the longer you travel and the more people in your group, the greater the opportunity for interpersonal squabbles and differences of opinion.

If your children don't get along very well at home, don't expect them to get along very well as you travel. Whatever problems exist between them will probably be exacerbated. Don't expect the family vacation to resolve the problems unless you are intentional in seeking a resolution. It's better to resolve problems before embarking on an adventure together.

Establish Rules Every bona fide exploration has a protocol and an administrative order. Establish the pecking order and certain behavioral rules for your family before you leave home. Make it clear that

- adults make final decisions, although input will be welcomed from children, and that final decisions are final.

- opinions are welcomed but only in the context of discussion, not argument.

- whining isn't allowed, and neither is pouting.

- obedience to parents is required; it could mean the difference between getting lost or injured and having a good, safe time.

Children sometimes attempt to manipulate a family vacation—forcing an early return home to their friends or an extra outing along the way—through misbehavior. After all, a parent's options for discipline are somewhat reduced when the troupe is traveling. Time-outs still work, however.

Defuse with a Time-Out and a Debate

When conflict erupts, call a halt to the anger, and try this line: "We'll discuss this after five minutes of silence. Think about your position. Think about the consequences. Think about what kind of compromise you are willing to make." And then set your watches for an all-family five-minute time-out.

Once conversation resumes, establish who will be the judge of a semiformal debate on the issue. The judge should ask first if there's a need to pursue a debate. The issue may have faded into unimportance by then. If raw anger still exists, call for an extended time-out of another five minutes. In pursuing a debate,

- allow for each person to state the case uninterrupted.

- allow for a rebuttal of each statement from each person.

- allow for closing remarks.

The judge should be permitted to ask questions of either party. Once the judge renders a decision, the decision should be considered final, with no "I told you so's," no one-upmanship, and no snide remarks or facial expressions.

Debrief Later Sometime later in the trip, perhaps a day or two later after all tempers have cooled sufficiently and the family is in a general good mood, you may want to return to the incident and explore it from an objective standpoint. Ask one of the parties involved to role-play as judge and state what he would have done in all fairness had he been hearing the case instead of being one of the debaters. Talk about how problems are resolved, what factors are considered in making problem-solving decisions, and why it's important to compromise on some points and stand firm on certain principles.

You can also debrief incidents that may occur between a family member and someone outside the family—perhaps an encounter with an obnoxious clerk or a road hog.

15 🚗 Take Your Manners with You

Common courtesy and good manners should not be left at home when the family goes on vacation. Take them with you! They'll make your trip easier.

Vacations are a good time for putting to the test what has been learned (ideally) at home:

- Saying "please," "thank you," and "no thank you"

- Opening doors for one another

- Volunteering to help

- Asking permission before forging ahead

- Using good table manners

- Saying "pardon me"

A child who displays good manners is made to feel welcome and special. A child who is made to feel welcome is a child who has more fun!

New Situations   From time to time on a family vacation, you may want to introduce your child to a formal event—a dinner in an elegant restaurant or a major theatrical performance or concert. Take clothes appropriate for the occasion. Prepare your child as much as you can in advance about how to behave in the new setting. Let your child participate in the process—using the appropriate silverware, ordering from an a la carte menu, checking a bill, leaving a tip, saying "pardon me" in crossing over ten seats of people, standing when an adult returns to the room or table, and so forth. The event can become a milestone in your child's growth toward social maturity.

Hotel and Motel Rooms   Insist that your child treat your hotel or motel room as he would if it was the guest room of a favorite older relative— no jumping on the beds, no loud noises, no major messes left behind. Leaving a room picked up is a great lesson in courtesy for your child to learn, and it will also make it easier for you to spot an item that you may have forgotten to repack.

Interruptions   One of the most basic courtesies a traveler can extend to another traveler is the privilege of silence. Be cautious about interrupting the reverie of another passenger in the car or the person who is gazing into a panorama of scenic beauty. Couple "don't interrupt me while I'm talking" with "don't interrupt me while I'm musing."

In times of excitement, let each family member have an opportunity to vent the emotional high. In conversations, don't let one family member hog the show.

16 🚗 Safety Precautions

Provide for your child's personal safety and the security of her possessions as much as you can.

Make certain that your child knows his full name, parents' names, his address (street, city, and state), and his phone number, including area code.

Mark your child's clothing with her name (especially last name). Attach to your child's personal bag a luggage tag showing name, address, and phone number.

Outfit your child with rubber-soled shoes for most outings. They'll grip slippery surfaces better.

Anytime your child is in a boat or enters a river or lake to water-ski, float in canoes or inner tubes, or engage in other water-sport activities in unsupervised swimming areas, see that he is wearing a life jacket. This rule applies no matter how capable a swimmer your child may be. You cannot be entirely sure of currents or debris, rocks, or tree limbs that may be just under the surface of the water.

Lost and Found   Designate a meeting place in case you become separated in what you know will be a busy area. Make the designated meeting place one that your child will remember readily and be able to ask directions to in case she loses sight of you. Show your child the place: "If we become separated, we'll meet right here where we are standing now, at the flagpole just inside the main gate." Don't just say, "If you get lost, ask for lost and found."

Stop and Sit Down   An effective procedure to teach your child is to stop moving and sit down if he becomes separated from you. Granted, you don't want him sitting down in a heavily trafficked walkway or in a road, but sitting on a curb is never inappropriate. Tell your child to say to any passerby who may question what he is doing, "I'm meeting my parents right here in just a couple of minutes."

Teach your child that it's much easier for you— being taller and able to move faster—to find your child than for your child to find you. The child who continues to wander, whether among the giant sequoia trees or the Disneyland palms, is likely to move farther away from you rather than closer to you.

Hold Hands and Stay Together   One of the best principles that a family can follow in a crowd is the one that all kindergarten teachers employ: hold hands and stay together. If you're in a crowded subway car, a packed shopping mall, or a teeming amusement park, reach for the hand of a family member. If your teen is embarrassed to hold hands with you, link arms or put your hand on the shoulder of a fellow family member. Stick together!

A Quarter and a Number to Call

Make sure that your child has the name of the place where you are staying—whether a campground name, a relative's name, or a motel name—and a phone number for the place written on a small piece of paper. Fold a quarter up in the piece of paper, and have the child stick both into a pocket or purse. Even though the coin or the information may never be needed, your child will have more confidence in exploring a new area with the knowledge that she can always find her way home, even a temporary home.

Mark Suitcases Well

In addition to the luggage tag on the outside of your suitcase, write your name and address on a piece of paper attached to the inside of your case. Include with that information the name and number of someone who should be notified in an emergency.

Valuables

Leave most valuables at home. Keep your camera with you at all times. Lock your room and car before leaving them, and store all valuables out of sight. Use traveler's checks rather than cash. Leave all local department store and little-used credit cards at home. If you must take valuables with you, take advantage of hotel or motel safes and security boxes. In traveling to foreign lands, pay special attention to your passports. Choose purses or personal bags that can be slung over the shoulder and head to carry cross-chested style.

A Dangerous Stranger or A Potential Friend? Some of the most interesting experiences you can have as a family will be opportunities to meet and talk with other families. Let your child know that it's OK to talk to people as you travel, but your child should never go anyplace with a person other than a family member, not even for just a moment. If your child becomes lost, he should never seek help from anyone who isn't clearly marked (by badge or uniform) as someone who holds proper authority, and he should never leave the place where you are, be it department store, city plaza, or ballpark. If someone attempts to nab your child, the best thing he can do is to yell at the top of his lungs, "Stranger! Stranger! Help me! Help me!"

Heed the Signs Most injuries on family outings could probably be avoided if all family members would heed warning signs that are posted. If the sign says, "No Trespassing," or "Don't Go Beyond This Line," stay where you are. There's plenty to explore within the limits.

17 🚗 A Family Identity

As a family traveling together, think of yourselves as your own self-contained tour group. Mark your identity!

Look-Alike Items You might want to consider

- matching T-shirts.

- matching visors or caps.

- a matching style of personal bags or beach totes.

Such uniforms come in handy when you are visiting a place that is likely to be very crowded. You'll keep track of one another easier. You are also likely to have total strangers come up to you and say, "What a great idea!" or "How clever of you!" Your look-alike item can be a good conversation opener.

Choose a look-alike item that is fun for all of you to wear. Be creative. Find something that is distinctive, colorful, and yet suitable to the occasion.

A Family Whistle Do you have a distinctive whistle for calling to one another? One can come in handy when you are faced with the challenge of locating a family member who has strayed from the pack. You might want to use your family vacation as an opportunity to create and test such a whistle. Make it an easy arrangement of notes that all family members can do.

Car Spotter Attach a bandana, colorful ribbon, or other waterproof item to your car antenna (unless it's the retractable kind, of course) to make it easier to find your vehicle in a large parking lot. Note the location of your car as you get out of it. Write the letters of your parking lot area on the back of a ticket stub or a receipt as quickly as you can, and tuck it into your wallet, purse, or the bottom of a shoe.

18 🚗 A Home Away from Home

Favorites from Home   Take along a few family icons to give your family a sense of home away from home wherever you travel.

You may want to include

- a small tape player and a few favorite cassette tapes. If you are like most families, each person has favorite music. If you can't all agree on an album or two of soothing music to play as you get ready for bed in the evening or as you change clothes in preparation for going out to dinner, pass the player and earphones around.

- a few favorite photos. You may want to include one of the family pet that was left behind, grandparents or other relatives that you see frequently when at home, or photos of your child's friends.

- your own pillow or lap blanket. A pillow or small blanket can be comforting, especially to a young child as she gets used to strange new beds and rooms. A pillow or blanket can also be a good item to take on planes or in cars to make travel naps a little easier to take.

- a night-light. A small night-light or two can help each family member feel more comfortable in strange surroundings and also be a safety device.

Personalizing Your Place Put away all advertising and motel or hotel information booklets, tent cards, and folders. Stick them in a drawer, and forget about them unless you truly need a service offered by the facility. If you don't have a smoker in your family, put away the ashtrays.

If you're going to be in a room for several days—especially at a family resort or in a suite hotel—and you are likely to be spending considerable time in your room, you may want to buy a bouquet of fresh flowers. If you are roombound for several hours and you don't feel as if you have enough light, request higher-wattage light bulbs or an extra lamp.

If you're going to be at an RV or tent campground for several days, find a way to make your new home feel personal and special—perhaps with an outdoor table centerpiece of pinecones gathered from the nearby forest floor, a jar of shells collected from the beach, or your lawn chairs from the patio at home.

The more comfortable you make your temporary home, the more at home and relaxed your child is likely to feel.

19 🚗 Personal Space

"Gimme space!"

That perhaps is one of the foremost laments heard on family vacations. Adults crave "alone" time. A child frequently does, too—especially a teenager. As best you can, provide literal and figurative space for each person in your family.

If Dad wants to take an early morning jog by himself, let him go!

If Mom wants an hour in the bathtub, let her soak, and take your child out to get picnic supplies at a nearby grocery store.

If a teenage son wants to sit on the balcony for a couple of hours listening to music through the earphones of his CD player, let him listen.

If a daughter would rather stay in the room and read her book than go for a swim, let her read (with instructions about keeping the door locked).

Making Room Make sure that each person has a space carved out in the vehicle in which you are traveling, and that each person has a designated space in any room where you are staying for the night.

If you're visiting with relatives or friends and

your child is spending the nights in a sleeping bag on the living room floor, find a daytime spot to which he can retreat and be with his things and thoughts.

The personal space you give to each person—which may be a drawer in a bureau, a nightstand by the bed, a three-cubic-foot space in the closet—should be inviolate. Let the person feel secure in stashing her personal things there. Let her be responsible for keeping that area neat and clean. Each person should have at least half a bed. Let your child curl up there and daydream, nap, or read in peace.

Sufficient Space   Too often families attempt to travel with too little space. Cramped conditions make for flared tempers. If you are a family of five or six, consider renting a van for your trip. Even a car that is advertised to seat six comfortably rarely can accommodate more than four people comfortably for a trip longer than a hundred miles.

Consider availing yourself of a suite motel or hotel as you travel. The rates are quite reasonable. You'll have two rooms—usually a living room space with a kitchen, dining table, and a sofa that converts to a bed, and then a bedroom and bath. These suites handle four or five people quite comfortably with sufficient space for everyone to have a corner to be alone. (Many suite hotels provide a free breakfast and have an indoor swimming pool and play area—all of which can add to a family member's sense of mobility and freedom within secure boundaries.)

Private Thoughts and Dreams   Everybody has a pensive day or moment periodically. If a family member isn't particularly talkative on any given day or part of a day, let it be so without comment or argument. (If there's a problem, of course, you'll want to ferret it out.) Let your child enjoy daydreams and imaginary moments as you travel along. If you say, "A penny for your thoughts," and the child says, "I'm not thinking anything," take that as your cue that your child wants to be alone in a world of his own making. His personal adventure in an imaginary space is just as important an experience as the journey you are taking together.

20 🚗 Share the Responsibilities

Spread out the workload so everyone can have fun.

Driving Chores If you have more than one driver in your family, take turns behind the wheel. Trade off every hour or every hundred miles. The trip will go by quicker for everybody.

Personal Suitcases Let each person be responsible for making certain that belongings are into the designated suitcase, that the suitcase is in the car at the end of a stay, and that all valuables or meltable items are taken out of a car and into a room overnight (including cassette tapes, photos, food, and candy). When the time comes to pack up and leave a room or campsite, more than one person should inspect the area for left-behind items, and all hands should be on deck to transport items to the car. The same goes for moving into a place for the night.

Each person should be 100 percent responsible for the personal bag (except for an infant or toddler, of course). Permit your child to have a suitcase of his own. Teach him how to pack it and how to keep items of clothing as wrinkle-free as possible. You may want to plan in advance and sort each day's clothing and underwear into large plastic lock-top bags. Other bags can be used for shoes, swimwear, nightwear, personal sundries, and accessories. Take along a large plastic laundry bag (or use one provided in a motel room) for storing dirty clothes. Each person should be responsible for putting dirty clothes into a designated laundry bag.

As a trip progresses, your child will end up with more clothes in the laundry bag and several empty plastic clothes bags. She can use these empty bags for stashing souvenirs collected along the way. This system of organization keeps a suitcase neat, helps shorten getting-ready time in the mornings, and allows for segregation of dirty garments as well as swimsuits that may still be damp.

Well-Ordered Space   Each person should be responsible for leaving a bathroom clean and presentable for the next person and for hanging up towels and washcloths. Each individual should be responsible for taking trash out of the personal area of the vehicle, tent, room, or van on a daily basis.

Personal Responsibility   Family members should have a sense of where they are—on the map, in the city, in the motel or hotel—and where the car is in the parking lot. Developing a keen sense of presence and alertness is a travel skill that's important for each person to develop. Use your family vacation as a time to help your child learn how to read maps, get a sense of direction, and develop the ability to look for landmarks that can help him identify where he is in relation to where he wants to be.

Help your child develop a sense of personal responsibility for her safety, health, and the security of her possessions. Show your child how to fold over and hold a shopping bag, carry a purse, carry a wallet, walk with boldness, and in general, avoid personal assault. Teach your child how to use public rest room facilities and drinking fountains in the most hygienic way possible. If you are traveling to areas where you are unsure of the availability of soap—and especially if you are traveling to a foreign country—tuck a small bar of soap into a small plastic bag in her personal bag. A small packet of tissues is also a good item to have along—one per person.

In many ways, a family vacation will only be as good as each family member makes it. If everyone takes primary responsibility for personal safety, health, and material goods, and also takes primary responsibility for a sense of fun and adventure, a truly wonderful experience can be had by all.

21 🚗 Stop a Lot

Be willing to stop frequently—even more frequently than your original definition of frequently!

The younger the child in your family, the more often you are likely to stop.

Don't stop grudgingly. Stop willingly. There's something to be gained at each stop—even if it's a good stretch and a yawn.

Always stop as quickly as you can if any member of your family

- states a need to use rest room facilities.

- is suffering from motion sickness. A child suffering from motion sickness is likely to need longer than a sixty-second stop. Walk around a bit with your child. Help her focus on fixed distant points.

- senses personal danger or has a sudden attack of fear. This is especially important to remember during times when you may be doing something that is a new experience for your child. Walking from stone to stone to cross the stream may be a piece of cake for you as an adult. It may seem like an extremely dangerous task to your child—indeed, it may be an extremely dangerous task for him!

- asks you to slow down. Little legs sometimes have difficulty keeping up. So do older legs!

- expresses an interest in taking a moment to enjoy an aspect of beauty. You certainly don't need to take advantage of every scenic-view turnout on your trip through the mountains or along the rocky shoreline, but take advantage of some of them.

Move Those Unused Limbs   Every time you stop the car for gasoline, a rest room break, a meal, or a "beauty break," get out of the car and stretch. Run in place a few steps. Do a few toe touches. Twirl your arms around, and do a few side bends and twists. Give your circulation a boost. If you've collected a few empty soda cans, spend a couple of minutes in playing one-on-one basketball as you toss the cans into the roadside bin. Take an opportunity to move and have fun at the same time.

A Shout Break   While traveling, some family members take a shout break at least once a day. They stop at a turnout or take an expressway exit ramp in an isolated area, all get out of the car, yell at the top of their lungs for a few minutes, and then get back in the car. In shouting, sometimes they use words—sometimes words they agree to shout in unison—and sometimes they simply resort to the international sound of release: a-a-a-a-g-g-h-h! The moment releases physical and emotional tension, adds a little interest to the trip, and gives them all something to laugh about.

What's an Extra Half Hour?   A father once became quite irritated at the number of times his children requested stops during their trip by car. He decided to add up all the minutes spent in unscheduled stops during the next day—his intention being, of course, to make a well-documented point. He timed each stop to the second and kept a running tally. At the end of the day, the unscheduled stops totaled thirty-two minutes. His conclusion? His children and wife had enjoyed a great day traveling. He had experienced a lousy day keeping track of the time. And in the end, he had to admit that the half-hour delay had kept them from the height of rush hour in a major city they had passed through on their journey.

Taking a few extra minutes to stop upon request rarely will make a major difference in your arrival time at a destination. It can, however, make all the difference in the world when it comes to how much you and others in your family enjoy your vacation.

22 🚗 Mark the Day's End

The end of a busy travel day should be marked in some way that is special and unique to your family. Most families have bedtime rituals when they are at home. Maintain those rituals as best you can while you are away, or adopt special travel rituals.

You may want to

- have one person read aloud a bedtime story to the rest of the family after you are all in pajamas.

- have a rip-roaring pillow fight or tickle fight.

- have a time of family prayer.

- sing a good-night song or say a bedtime poem together.

- read a passage from the Bible or from your favorite collection of positive stories and quotes.

- share hugs and kisses all around.

- do any combination of the above!

A Quiet Note   In some way, bring closure to the day. In so doing, you are giving your child permission to be quiet and go to sleep.

Your child may perceive the first few days of a vacation as a party or even a slumber party. Talking can go long into the night after an especially wonderful or exciting day. Let your child know that when the lights are turned out and the final "good nights" are said, it's time for quiet and sleep.

A Positive Note   You'll also find that having a good end to the day is a way of putting each day to rest in the memory on a positive note, even if the day has been filled with unexpected, unwelcome, or even unpleasant moments. The day's end is a good time to

- say "I'm sorry" and ask for forgiveness.

- talk about what went wrong and make a decision to do better the next day.

- recall the bad time and laugh about it.

- sift the positive moments from the negative ones.

Marking the end of the day in a positive way can keep hurt and anger from building day to day. It is a way to build relationships and let the night heal wounds that would otherwise fester.

23 🚗 Laughs and Hugs

The need for lots of laughs and hugs on a trip cannot be overstated. There's simply no substitute for either if a family is to survive, and enjoy, a vacation!

A Hug a Day Start and end each day with hugs all around. Periodically during the day, give each child a hug. It may be just an arm-around-the-shoulder hug as you walk from exhibit to exhibit or a surprise-from-behind hug as you stop on a hike. Take your child's hand and skip, or link arms with your teenager as you stroll a city street after dinner. Give each child a sense of connectedness to you and to others in your family.

A Laugh a Day Find something to laugh about every day. The best laughter, of course, is spontaneous. Sometimes, however, the laugh pump needs to be primed. What may begin as forced laughter frequently turns into a lighter-hearted mood that can make genuine spontaneous giggles a possibility.

Avoid these don'ts in laughter:

- Don't laugh *at* a member of your family. If the family member isn't laughing, too, stop the guffawing. At the same time, encourage in your children an ability to laugh at themselves. The best way to do that is to let them see that you can laugh at yourself!

- Avoid laughing at things that are rude or crude. Life has plenty of mishaps, miscues, and missteps without anybody having to resort to the vulgar.

- Never laugh at a person's race, culture, disability, or weight. You'll only be reinforcing attitudes that you may wish you could undo later.

Here are several ways to get laughter started:

- Take along a joke or riddle book. Your response may be groaning instead of laughing, but the net effect is generally a brighter mood.

- Have a three-minute tickle fest. Make every person a fair and equal target. Decide on certain rules in advance, such as parts of the body not to touch, areas of the room to avoid for safety reasons, and so forth. Set a timer or alarm (the digital ones in many motel rooms work just fine for this!). Don't exceed the three-minute limit, but get as many laughs going as possible.

- Ask your children to dream up funny skits as your evening entertainment. Encourage them to come up with humorous costumes or props to enhance the comedic aspects of their plot.

- Learn some new tongue twisters.

- Play the old stare-into-another-person's-eyes-and-try-not-to-laugh game. It's a surefire way to evoke laughter.

- Another surefire approach is to play "head on the tummy." Each person lies on the back with the head on another person's stomach. It only takes one person to start laughing— or to attempt to stifle laughter—for you all to be in a gale of laughs. (This is best, of course, with a family of at least four people.)

- Just start laughing. Someone else will soon be laughing at your laughing. Laughter— even for no apparent reason—is contagious.

Smiles Count, Too Pass along smiles of all varieties—from subtle and secretive to wide and Cheshire-cat style. Smiles, like yawns and laughs, spread quickly from person to person.

Share your smiles and laughter with clerks, waiters, and fellow traveling companions. You'll all have a better time, and you're likely to get better service. People like to be with people and to serve those who obviously enjoy being together.

24 🚗 A Family Fun Bag

Surprise! Pack a small bag or suitcase of items that are just for fun. Throw in such items as these:

- Joke and riddle books

- A storybook (that might take you several days to read aloud as a family)

- A ball or sponge ball (softball or football)

- A Frisbee

- A sack of marbles

- A sack of jacks and a rubber ball

- A yo-yo or two

- A jump rope

- An extra box of crayons and a couple of coloring books (one teenager spent hours on a family vacation coloring in a book of intricate designs—something she wouldn't have been caught dead doing at home with her friends, but she enjoyed it immensely as an on-the-road activity)

- A few magazines, books, puzzle books, or games

If you run out of ideas, take a trip to a bookstore or toy shop. Even if you don't buy anything, you'll probably be reminded of things that you have at home that you might take.

It may be fun for you to keep the contents of this bag a secret and then periodically on your trip come up with a surprise that leads to activity and fun.

Indoors and Outdoors   Have a balance between items that are for indoor and outdoor use. Take along items that won't melt in the heat of an automobile trunk. In choosing toys and games to take along, choose ones that don't require batteries, and that have few breakable parts or pieces. If you are taking along a board game, make certain you have all the pieces before you leave home. Choose magnetic or Peg-Board games whenever possible; they are more trip-hardy.

Prior to leaving for your trip, make an inventory of everything you are putting in your family fun bag, and then consult the list periodically to check that all items you've taken out have been returned.

25 🚗 Swap Stories

Entertain yourselves with stories as you travel by car, plane, or ship.

Books The story may be one that you read aloud from a book to other members of your family. Let each person capable of reading take a turn. You can read as you travel (as long as the reader doesn't suffer from motion sickness, of course), during an after-lunch rest break in a park, or before bedtime. Choose a story that has lots of action, good characterizations and twists of plot that will yield thought-provoking conversations, and plenty of description.

Stick to the classic children's books and you won't go wrong. The stories by Robert Louis Stevenson are particularly good for this activity: *Treasure Island, Travels on a Donkey,* and *Kidnapped.* You might also want to consider *Robinson Crusoe* by Daniel Defoe, *Gulliver's Travels* by Jonathan Swift, *The Adventures of Sherlock Holmes* by Sir Arthur Conan Doyle, or *Green Dolphin Street* by Elizabeth Goudge.

If you pick a book that is longer than you will be able to complete during your trip, either start the reader's theater portion of your trip a few days in advance of your departure, or continue the saga upon your return home. You may find that you've created a new family tradition!

(Choose materials suitable to the age of your child. Keep reading times short—no more than ten minutes at a time.)

Tapes   An alternative to reading books in the car is listening to books that have been recorded professionally. Check out a couple of books on tape from your local library. You'll probably be amazed at the variety available to you. You may even want to check out an instructional course of some type or an inspiring set of tapes on building self-esteem or a winning attitude.

Tapes are especially enjoyed by a teenager. Even if she professes to be uninterested in a book or topic initially, she's likely to be interested by the time the first tape ends.

Magazines   Buy your child a magazine prior to your departure, and give it as a gift when you sense your child is getting bored.

Create-a-Tale   You can have a fun activity and a good learning experience in playing Create-a-Tale with your family. One person starts telling a story. The person must give a vivid description when introducing a new character or place. Let the person spin the tale awhile and then pass it off to another member of the family, who is then free to twist and develop the plot as he sees fit, to introduce new characters, or to jump forward or backward in time.

You may want to tape your story for later reference and laughter. Create-a-Tale tapes are great souvenirs from family vacations. Their value increases with time.

Tall Tales Pick a category and let each person in the vehicle tell a tale. You might start with one of these categories:

- My Most Embarrassing Moment
- The Most Awful Thing I Can Imagine
- My Most Terrifying Moment
- The Scariest Story I've Ever Heard

Encourage each person to elaborate as much as possible on why it was or would be the "most." These tales often give rise to good conversations about fears in general and how to confront them and deal with them.

26 🚗 Recall the Past

A family vacation is a good time to reinforce family memories and experiences from the past, and to build a stronger sense of family identity and heritage.

Grandma and Grandpa Stories Give your child an insight into what life was like when his grandparents were children, how and where they grew up, how they met and married, and what life was like in the home you grew up in. Many children are amazed to think about the fact that Grandma was once as young as they are and that Grandpa didn't always have gray hair.

Your History Tell your child about your past experiences in life to the extent that your child can relate to them and find them interesting. Don't burden your child with your failures or painful experiences. Do share information about places you've been, people you've met, and successes you've had.

Your Child's Early Years Share anecdotes from your child's baby and toddler years: first words, first steps, first likes and dislikes. Funny, warm, heart-touching personal stories give your child a sense that she has always been loved and wanted. There's no advantage in telling your child how painful childbirth was. There's great advantage in telling your child how frantic her dad was in trying to get you to the hospital and how wonderful you felt when she was born!

Past Family Experiences   Play a conversation game called Do You Remember the Time . . . ? A child tends to forget experiences in the past, and some experiences you think your child would never remember may be deeply etched in memory. Help your child see that the past has had good times and bad times, but that in the overall mix, you're still together, still traveling, and still glad for your child's presence in your life.

Q & A Times   Give your child the freedom to ask you questions about your life and the lives of his grandparents and aunts and uncles. Answer the questions as honestly and clearly as you can. If you wish not to answer a particular question, let your child know that you'll tell him someday but that now isn't the time for that answer. Move on to the next question.

Nostalgia   As you travel together as a family, you may frequent old haunts, hometowns, or cities that hold special meaning for you as parents. A sweet trip down memory lane for you is likely to be a royal bore for your child, however, unless you augment the experience with stories that capture the imagination. Don't just describe the way things used to look; tell about the way you felt back then and what happened in various places. Describe some of your friends or the people you knew in the old neighborhood and what they did that stands out in your memory. To a child, your junior high school or the house you lived in when you were six is just another old building. Stories about you will make the excursion enjoyable.

27 ⊕ Share Your Music

Have a listening hour as you travel. Let each person in the family contribute ten to fifteen minutes' worth of music. To be able to do this, of course, each person will need to bring along a few favorite cassette tapes.

You may detest your child's selection of music—and he yours—but you can force yourselves to listen to it in the course of building a relationship and understanding across the generations.

Between musical segments,

- talk about the lyrics of the songs that have been chosen—either those you have just heard or those you are about to hear. Let the person playing the music set up the selections in the most favorable light.

- ask questions about or tell about the artist who made the recording. What other songs is the person noted for writing, singing, or playing?

- talk about the style or genre of music and various qualities that it possesses across artists and over the years.

If you are interested in learning something about the music your child likes, your child will be far more interested in learning more about what you like.

Turn that Radio Dial   If you haven't brought along tapes, try sampling what is available on the radio in a particular area. You may find something truly unusual, such as hearing country music on a radio station in northern Maine or a jazz concert from a station in New Mexico. Again, limit your listening time to ten or fifteen minutes per station sampled. Any person in the car can listen for that long.

It's a good idea before extending a listening time to take a family vote: "Shall we hear more of this?" If there's a "no" vote, move on. Sometimes, however, you'll find that your child truly is interested in the talk show or the oldies-but-goodies station that captured your attention. If that's the case, give yourself an extra fifteen-minute treat.

Have Your Own Sing-Along   Teach your child some of the lyrics you learned and loved as a child. Sing old traditional hymns and choruses that you sang as a teenager but that your teenager may never have heard. Share how certain songs evoke specific feelings or memories.

Let your child, in turn, teach you some of the songs that she has learned in school or that she enjoys singing in the shower. Update your repertoire!

28 ⚗ Verbal Travel Games

When in doubt about what to talk about, turn to some of the traditional family travel games.

I Spy Take turns spying out unusual things along the way and giving clues that eventually reveal what has been spotted. As a variation on this game, ask family members to keep track of how many times they see a certain word during a given time period (perhaps a half hour) or until your arrival at a specified stop. Look for words such as these:

- *City*

- *Mart*

- *New*

- *Land*

The word might be part of or hyphenated to another word. The first person to spot the word on a sign or vehicle gets a point. The winner is the person with the most points at the end of the time period or end of the travel segment.

A to Z   Choose from any number of topics, for example:

- "I'm so hungry I could eat a . . ."
- "If I could go anywhere in the whole world, I'd go to . . ."
- "If I could have any animal I wanted as a pet, I might choose a . . ."
- "If I was Heidi and dressing for my trip, I might find that I had as part of my clothing an . . ."

Fill in the blanks with the names of items from *A* to *Z*—in other words, from abalone to zucchini, Australia to Zambia, armadillo to zebra, apron to zipper. Go in rotation from family member to family member. A person who fails to come up with a word within ten seconds (or any given time frame you choose) is out of the game. The last person in the game wins.

As a variation on this game, look for words that begin with the letters of the alphabet on billboards and signs.

License Plate Mania   See how many different states you can spot while reading license plates. Keep track of the state names you see. What is the highest number of vehicles from different states you've encountered on the road in a given day?

29 🚗 The Traveling Puppet Show

Make up your own puppet theater, and take your show on the road.

By Car Before your trip by car, gather together a few small brown paper bags and a big box of crayons. Add them to your fun bag. As you travel, let your child decorate the bags as puppets. Create characterizations for the puppets, and then make up stories starring them.

By Plane If you are traveling by plane, avail yourself of the air-sickness bags in the seat pockets directly in front of you, and have each family member create a puppet for use either on the plane or upon arrival. (If you don't find bags, ask a flight attendant for a couple.)

One young mother used such puppets to stop her toddler twins from crying on a flight that had left them bored. She sent the puppets on an imaginary journey out of the plane and onto the clouds where they bounced on the clouds and chased each other all over the heavens, sliding down an occasional rainbow and jumping in fright as they dodged lightning bolts. With a puppet on each hand, she held them spellbound for more than half an hour—at which point, the pilot was well into his descent.

Puppets open up a child's feelings and innermost thoughts. They capture the imagination of a child and give voice to ideas your child may not have realized he had.

Finger puppets and socks are alternatives to paper bags.

30 🚗 Lists and Logs

Captains keep logs, as any "Star Trek" fan will tell you (from either generation of programs). So can the adventurers in your plane, ship, car, van, train compartment, or RV.

Note the Usual and the Unusual Build upon the things that your child notices along the way. Are the names of the gas stations different in this part of the nation or world? Do the grocery stores have different names? Suggest that your child keep a list of all the names spotted. Here are some categories to consider:

- Names of places that have a proper name in them or place names that end in "ville"

- Names for various types of roadways, from thruways to boulevards

- Brands of gasoline

- Types of cars

- Names of all the waterways (creeks, rivers, lakes, bays, inlets) that you cross by bridge

Trip Journals Keep track of your starting and stopping mileage each day. And as part of your vehicle log, you may also want to record other items.

Number of gallons of gasoline used Give your child a good math exercise. Ask her to figure the average miles per gallon for a given tank of gasoline and also to keep a running tally of your gasoline consumption and average mileage per gallon.

Number of miles traveled compared to number of hours on the road On which stretches of road did you make the best time?

Unusual scenery or interesting historical sites along the way Ask your child to pretend that he is keeping a log that might be used by others who are planning a similar trip. Point out that travelers in centuries past referred to the logs of their predecessors to inspire and guide their journeys.

Expense Accounting Keep track of all the money you spend on the trip—as individuals and as a family. Calculate your least expensive and most expensive days. Where was your money best spent?

Consider these to be official family documents—master logs of your family vacation. They might be kept in addition to any personal diaries your child may keep. They'll make for interesting conversations through the years.

31 🚗 Travel Through Time and Space

As you travel through a particular region, on a waterway, or over a certain trail, take an imaginary trip through time with your family.

Time Past Ask yourselves, "What was it like in this part of the world one hundred years ago? Two hundred years ago? Five hundred years ago? If we had been tourists then, who would we have been and how would we have traveled?"

Ask, "What would have been here that isn't here now? What's here now that wouldn't have been here then?"

Ask, "Why do you suppose people built a city here?" (Look for a river and explore the reason that most major cities are built close to rivers or on bays.)

Time Future Turn the clock forward and ask yourselves, "What do you think it will be like in this area a hundred years from now? Two hundred years from now? Five hundred years? If we could be tourists then, who do you think we'd be and how would we travel from place to place?"

Ask, "What will be obsolete by then?"

Time travel can really set your child's imagination on fire. A number of spin-off conversations are likely—from conservation and ecology to the history of transportation and the entire realm of cultural geography.

Space Travel   Don't think in terms of outer as much as in terms of through the center of the earth. Ask, "If we dug a tunnel through the earth, where would we come out? What would travel in that place be like?"

Or ask, "If we could suddenly be transported five hundred miles due south, where would we be? What would we likely be doing if we had taken a vacation to that place?" Extend yourself in other directions and other distances.

You'll need to have a world or national atlas with you for this travel activity, but in the course of playing such games, your child can learn a great deal of geography without even a hint of playing school.

Consider it your family version of "Where in the World Is Carmen Sandiego?"

32 🚗 Travel Talk

It's one thing to talk as you travel; it's another to talk about travel and travelers. Here are some ideas for conversations and discussions as you roll, gallop, or fly along together.

Famous Travelers Several weeks prior to your trip, encourage your child to read a book or two about a famous traveler—perhaps Charles Lindbergh's story or stories about Magellan or the Apollo astronauts.

Ask your child to share the stories he has read. Put your family—by means of the imagination—on the ship or in the plane that your child describes. What would it have been like to be a silent passenger on the voyage or flight? How long did the journey take? What did it accomplish?

Note that most famous travelers took their journeys when they were fairly young, and that their families rarely went with them. What would it have been like to be part of the family that had to stay at home?

What would it be like to go someplace where no one you had ever heard about had been? Are such places left? Where are they? How would a person get there?

Did the explorers truly discover a place, or were they just the first of their nation or culture to visit it?

Famous Trips and Routes   As you travel across the country or from state to state, talk about the route you are taking. Why was the road built where it is? What natural formations and geographic conditions come into play? Where are the roadways in relation to the farming areas, the rivers, and the railways? Why do freeways seem to avoid small towns? When looking at the U.S. as a whole, why do there seem to be more major east-west roads than north-south ones? Why are there more roads in the eastern than in the western regions of the U.S.?

Modes of Transportation   You may want to sample a new form of transportation on your family vacation—either as your principal mode of travel to your destination point or as a brief side trip along the way. Has your child ever been on a train apart from one at an amusement park? Has your child ever been on a ferry or a ship? Has your child ever been in a hot air balloon, a helicopter, or a small plane? Has your child ever ridden a horse? This may be the trip to try a new method of transportation. You'll have lots to talk about as a result!

33 🚗 Switch Positions

Don't stay glued to one seat the entire trip. Although you may have a given place in a car or van, a vacation is a time to try looking at the world from a little different perspective.

Up Front Give every person a turn sitting in the front with the driver (except for an infant or toddler in a safety seat that is better left in the backseat). The view from the front seat is different and far more encompassing and vivid than the one seen from the backseat.

Let every person have a turn at a window seat, especially if you are traveling by air.

Rotate positions periodically throughout the day. Divide your time, and with the exception of the driver's seat, allow for every person to sit in every position available in the vehicle at some time during the day.

As a parent, you'll have a better understanding of what your child is experiencing if you sit in the back, too. The child will have a greater sense of responsibility for the trip if he's sitting in the front with the driver for a couple of hours a day.

Assignments   Let an assignment go with each position. For example, the person sitting in the passenger seat may be responsible for helping the driver look for road signs, tuning the radio, or managing snacks or beverages. The person behind the driver may be the trip log keeper. The person in the other side of the backseat may be the official navigator and map reader.

In shifting positions, also shift roles.

The trip will take on a whole new character as each person shares more responsibility for the trip's success and comes to see the world through the eyes of fellow passengers.

If you are fortunate enough to be traveling with children or relatives who all have driver's licenses, you'll truly be able to make the rounds within your vehicle!

34 🚗 Have Picnics

If you are taking a family vacation that involves several days of automobile travel, consider opting for picnics at lunchtime.

You can take along the old family picnic basket and stock it with some basics before you leave home—disposable plates, napkins, flatware, cups —and perhaps various food items, such as bottles or cans of soda, chips, cookies, and crackers. Then as you travel, look for a grocery outlet, and stop to pick up what you might need to make sandwiches and perhaps a small bag of ice and a few pieces of fruit.

You can make your sandwiches as you travel— something of a rolling picnic—or you can stop at a local city park, an area lake or riverbank, or a designated roadside rest area or picnic ground.

On the Move Picnics provide several unique opportunities to the family on the move:

- Everybody can pitch in and help make lunch, providing activity and a sense of responsibility for your child.

- The food tends to be fresher and lower in calories, cholesterol, fat, and sodium than many fast-food meals; family members with dietary restrictions are more easily accommodated, too.

- The time spent preparing and eating is comparable to that for a fast-food meal, but with a picnic the time is flexible.

- If you stop for your picnic at a place of beauty or a place of historical significance, you'll have a better view and environment than the interior of a restaurant and have an opportunity to breathe some fresh air.

- You'll learn a little about how the people in another town or city live and discover the amazing variety among grocery outlets from place to place.

- You'll have a unique opportunity to try local specialties. You may want to pick up what you need at an ethnic bakery or delicatessen.

- You'll have a greater variety of choices than the typical burger, fries, and cola meal, although you will probably also have to do some compromising as a family.

- The money you spend will probably be about the same as that spent on a fast-food restaurant meal but will likely be considerably less than a restaurant meal.

- You don't have to worry about how you look or how you are dressed. Picnics can be as casual as you want them to be!

Picnic leftovers make splendid late-afternoon snacks, and in some cases, provisions can last until the following morning. Be cautious, however, in your storage of perishables. Keep meats, cheeses, and items such as mayonnaise thoroughly chilled.

In stopping for a picnic, of course, you can have the added advantage of a break from car travel. Give your child a chance to run around and explore a new area.

The Picnic Breakfast The members of one family regularly plan picnic breakfasts. They purchase bananas, juice, and milk as they travel, and they take with them a couple of large boxes of cereal. They travel an hour before eating, which gives everyone in the family time to thoroughly wake up. Picnic grounds are generally vacant during their 8:00 to 9:00 A.M. picnic time. The children have time for a few minutes of play that helps them cope with the rest of the morning on the road.

35 🚗 Navigational Skills

A family vacation is a great time to teach your child how to read maps of all types, read a compass, mark a trail, and become adept at receiving and giving directions.

Map Reading Take along an up-to-date road map. You may want to give one to your child, too. Mark the route you intend to take.

When you enter a theme park, a campground with hiking trails, or even a shopping mall, stop to get oriented with the maps that are provided.

Three-dimensional and illustrated maps make fun souvenirs, too.

Compass Reading Take along a compass, even if you aren't hiking. It's easy to get turned around in a city and think you are walking in one direction when you are headed the opposite way. A child enjoys watching a compass while riding in a car. Compasses are also fun to take to view special sights—whether it's overlooking the Grand Canyon or looking out the windows at the top of the Sears Tower. Teach your child how to transfer compass readings to a map.

Trail Marking Paths in a state park, malls, and theme parks have a great deal in common—the need for finding visible, readily identifiable landmarks in order to have a sense of direction and position. Help your child learn how to mark a trail by stopping occasionally and getting her bearings in all four directions. Take note of certain geographic features or signs.

Ask periodically, "Which way would you go if you wanted to get back to the main gate (or to your campsite or vehicle)?"

Giving and Receiving Directions One of the most important skills your child can learn in life is the ability to give and receive clear, precise, and simple directions. Vacation time is a good time to build or reinforce those skills, especially when it comes to navigation. Here are some basic skills to teach:

- Give directions in terms of north, south, east, or west rather than left, right, up, or down. For example, say, "Go two blocks north, and it will be on the east side of the street," as opposed to saying, "Go two blocks up, and it will be on your left."

- Affirm directions by using the word *correct* rather than *right*. Right is a direction!

- Consult the scale of a map before stating how far away something is likely to be. Going an inch up the map may be traveling five miles or twenty.

• Always have a backup plan in mind, especially if the road you had planned to travel is under repair or a detour is necessary because of an accident.

Many maps give mileage summaries between designated points. Let your child total the number of miles you hope to travel before your next stop and translate those miles into minutes for you— given the average speed you are able to travel on that road. The math exercise will be fun.

36 🚗 Sensible Eating

A vacation is not a time for ignoring basic nutritional needs. Quite the contrary! A family vacation is an important time for stressing solid eating habits.

Plenty of Fluids   Insist that every member of the family drink plenty of liquids—even if it means an additional stop or two a day. Take along a container that each person can fill with ice and water at the beginning of the day. Avoid drinking too many sodas. Not only will you be cutting down on sugar and caffeine, but you'll be limiting sodium intake and, thus, uncomfortable water-retention feelings. If you have any questions about the purity of the water in an area, purchase bottled water (making sure that it is properly sealed).

It's especially important that you drink lots of water if you are exerting a great deal of energy (such as hiking or spending hours playing water polo) or if you are traveling in areas where it is hot or very humid.

Avoid Junk Food   Fast foods and highly processed foods tend to be loaded with fat and sugar.

They may be good for quick energy, but in the long haul of a trip, they'll leave you feeling more lethargic and uncomfortable.

Seek Out Fresh Fruits and Vegetables and Salads   Insist that family members have at least one meal a day that includes fresh vegetables or salads. French fries don't count! Provide unsweetened fruit juice or pieces of fruit at lunch, breakfast, or an afternoon snack.

Think Light   If you are traveling long distances by car or van, eat lighter than you would at home. You'll feel more comfortable with the long hours of sitting.

Vitamins   If you normally take vitamins as a family, take them along on your trip. Use clearly labeled containers so that medicines and vitamins don't become confused.

Snacks   Provide for nutritious midmorning and late-afternoon snacks. This is especially important if you are engaged in high-energy activities or if you are eating light meals while traveling.

A Hot Meal   In my travels as a child, Mom always insisted that we stop for one hot meal a day, even if it was just a bowl of soup and a roll. Fast food didn't count; from Mom's perspective, that food was always lukewarm and precooked. Nutritionally, there was no need for a meal to be cooked. In the course of a multiday trip by car, however, there were several good reasons to stop for a hot meal. First, such a meal meant that we would be out of our vehicle long enough to have a real break from the motion and confines of the car. Second, a hot meal meant the opportunity to be waited on. I'm sure that was a treat for Mom. Third, a hot meal kept us attuned to our normal at-home schedule, which always included at least one hot meal a day. Fourth, there was a sense of comfort about a hot meal—a feeling of inner warmth that left each of us not only comfortably full but satisfied.

The Reward of Good Health Following good nutritional habits on the road results in better physical health and better emotional health—with fewer sugar highs and lows that can manifest themselves as hyperactivity, lethargy, or a general case of grumpiness.

37 🚗 Take Along a Repair Kit

Take along a small bag—perhaps a gallon-sized resealable plastic bag—that can suffice as an all-purpose repair kit.

Here are some items you may want to include in it:

- Extra-strength glue

- Spot remover (and a small sponge)

- An extra pair or two of shoelaces

- A tiny screwdriver for tightening glasses or sunglasses

- A simple sewing kit that includes several needles and colors of thread (white and black can always do in an emergency), a few extra buttons or hooks and eyes of various sizes, several pieces of elastic, and a few patches

- A small roll of masking or packing tape

- A Swiss Army knife or similar style knife with lots of gadgets

- A can opener and bottle opener (if not a part of your Swiss Army knife)

- A compass

You just never know.

Extra Keys Although technically not in the category of repair, an extra set of keys can save the day and possibly your trip. Have at least two sets of keys to the car and perhaps a third one hidden in a small magnetic container located somewhere under the vehicle. (Remember, thieves know all the obvious places!) Also, have an extra set of keys to suitcases or containers that you are taking with you, even if you don't intend to lock them.

Take a set of house keys with you. Fewer things are more frustrating than arriving home exhausted at the end of a vacation and discovering that no one has a key to the house!

Car Emergency Kit The vehicle in which you are traveling should have a basic emergency kit with flares, a "Help" sign to put in a back window, jumper cables, and a lightweight blanket to use should a person suffer from shock, exposure, or frostbite. Your vehicle should also have an empty one-gallon metal gasoline can and another clean empty container designated for water only. Check your spare tire to make sure it's in good working order, and see that the jack is properly stored in the trunk. If you have a vehicle that may be considered exotic in the area where you will be traveling, you may want to take along a couple of extra spark plugs, a fan belt, or any other item that you'd hate to have to back order.

Radio   Take along a small radio, which may be part of a cassette player. Pack plenty of batteries. You may find this to be very important if you are traveling to an area that frequently has severe storms. (If you are flying to your destination point, you may want to check your radio, tape player, and other electronic devices. You'll have less delay in getting through airport security checkpoints. While you may listen through earphones to a tape or CD player on an airplane at any time, the airlines now discourage or prohibit the use of radios and laptop computers during takeoffs and landings.)

38 🚗 Take Along a First-Aid Kit

Take with you a basic but adequate first-aid kit that includes these items:

- A thermometer

- An assortment of bandages, including gauze and tape

- Pain medication

- An antiseptic

- Cotton swabs and cotton balls

- A large clean handkerchief in case you need to make a temporary sling

- Insect repellent

- Sunscreen

- Cold medication

- Diarrhea medication

- Antacids

You may want to pack all of your supplies in a plastic resealable bag and then put the entire kit in a cloth ice-pack bag.

If you are traveling to a foreign country or are planning on some serious back-trails hiking, you may also want to take water purification tablets.

Instructions   Make sure that you have a first-aid booklet should you need a quick refresher about what to do in an emergency. You may want to review first-aid procedures with your child as you make your trip to an outdoor destination point —such as a lakeside, oceanside, or mountain environment. Review general safety precautions as well.

If you suffer periodically from ear infections, a particular skin disorder, or other similar ailment, take the medications you normally use with you. If you need them, you'll be very glad you have them.

Prescriptions   Take plenty of any prescription medication you need, including insulin. (Take a couple of extra days' worth—you never know when you might be delayed.)

Take along a copy of your written prescriptions, too. If you are taking a round of antibiotics or other medicine, take that medication with you, and continue to take the full dosage prescribed.

Phone Numbers   Tuck into your first-aid kit the phone numbers for your pharmacist, pediatrician, family doctor or internist, dentist, and any other health care professional you tend to see on a regular basis, such as an allergist.

ID Bracelets If you have a major disease or medical condition that could warrant immediate medical attention—such as diabetes, hemophilia, or an extremely allergic reaction to bee stings— wear your ID bracelet at all times during your vacation.

A Hat Every member of the family should take along a hat. Not only does a hat help a traveler through bad-hair days, but a hat is an important piece of equipment to have at any time you are planning to be in the sun. If you are planning on doing any bicycling, take your helmet along.

An Extra Pair If you wear glasses or contact lenses, take along the supplies you need and an extra pair of your most recent prescription. If you wear a hearing aid, pack extra batteries.

39 🚗 Leave Home in Good Working Order

It's great to be able to fix things, medicate ailments, and circumvent emergencies during a vacation. It's even more important that you leave home in good working order.

Healthy If a member of your family is ill, postpone your trip for a day or two. Otherwise, your sick family member will be all the more miserable as he attempts to get well in a strange environment, and he may well infect other family members who will get sick as the trip progresses.

The Vehicle Have your car, van, or RV thoroughly checked before you leave town. The same goes for any boats, motor scooters, or bicycles you may be taking with you. If you question whether your vehicle is adequate for the trip, consider renting a vehicle. Your trip may need to be a day or two shorter to balance off the additional expense, but the trade-off may mean the difference between an enjoyable time at the lakeside bay and a vacation spent hovering around the bays of an auto shop.

Clothing Before the trip, check that seams are sewn, buttons and other fasteners are secure, and all zippers are working smoothly. Have garments dry-cleaned or laundered well in advance of your departure time. Check shoes and sandals to make certain that straps are tight, heels and soles are adequate. Don't wait to the last minute to locate the accessories you want to take with you. As you envision an outfit you want to take, locate and pack jewelry, ribbons, hair bows and clips, belts, scarves, and other accessories in a plastic bag.

Gear If you are camping or are taking along specialized sporting equipment, gather together all the elements you need, and see that each piece of equipment is in good condition.

Pets Don't expect a house sitter to doctor your ailing pet. If your pet needs medical attention on a regular daily basis or several times a day, leave it in a kennel where it can be properly treated by a veterinarian. If you are taking a pet with you, get it checked prior to the trip, and take with you all the supplies you will need.

Your House Don't ask a person to house-sit for you if you know that the heating or air-conditioning isn't working, you have a major plumbing problem, or doors and windows can't be secured. Make sure your security alarm systems are in good order, and arrange to have the mail and newspaper delivery stopped while you are away (or arrange for someone to pick up these items on a daily basis).

Set lights on timers. Leave precise instructions for the care of your house plants. You'll feel better if you come home to a house that is clean, with the dishes washed. Unplug or turn off all electrical appliances. Disconnect your computer and other sensitive electronic devices in case of a major power surge, loss of power, or storm damage.

Part of leaving home in good order is also leaving a copy of your itinerary with those at your place of employment, those who may be caring for your home or pets, and close friends or relatives who may be concerned about your safety as you travel.

40 🚗 Day or Night?

Nighttime As you plan your trip, ask several questions: Can our child sleep well in the car? Do we have sufficient room to provide a safe place for our child to sleep as we travel? Do both adults see well—and drive well—at night?

If so, you may want to load the car or van in the late afternoon and, after dinner, have your child don nightwear and climb aboard. This is a good way to get lots of miles covered before boredom sets in, and it is a means of travel especially suited to a family with an infant or toddler. A child who suffers from motion sickness also seems to do better with night travel.

One adult should stay with the child during any stop for gasoline or coffee, and for safety purposes, both adults should stay awake and be alert during the entire travel time. If you need sleep, pull over to the side of the road and take a nap. If you choose to travel at night, allow yourself sufficient rest during the next couple of days at your destination point. If at all possible, take a shower and a nap upon arrival.

Red-eye flights can be a good way of covering

long distances in the air. Overnight trains can also provide a fun family vacation experience.

Extra-Early Departures   One family enjoyed taking one-day excursions to several different locations within a two-hundred-mile radius of home. The parents would get the kids up at 4:00 or 5:00 A.M.—awakening them just enough so they could toddle out to the car in their pajamas—and they'd head out. The kids were nearly always asleep before they passed the city limits. By the time the kids awoke a couple of hours later, the travel time was half over. After the kids had changed clothes in the backseat of the car and the family had stopped for breakfast, they were ready to see landmarks prior to arrival at opening time of the national park, zoo, or amusement park. They'd enjoy a full day of sightseeing and activity, and then after supper, the kids would put back on their pajamas and go to sleep. Mom and Dad had long days, of course.

Decision-Making Factors When deciding whether to travel during the day or night, you may also want to factor in

- the direction in which you are traveling. Are you smarter to leave early in the morning and let the sun set while you are having dinner rather than drive into the setting sun for a couple of wearisome hours?

- road conditions. If the roads are in poor condition or have lots of curves, or if the route has detours and stretches of construction, you may want to travel during daylight hours to feel more secure. If you will be traveling a lonely stretch of road, you'll probably feel more secure if you have a cellular phone or CB radio with you should you choose to travel at night.

- the weather. It's easier to travel by day if the weather is bad. On the other hand, if you see on a national weather report that a storm is headed your way, you may be wise to drive at night to avoid the full force of it.

- the climate and scenery. You may be more comfortable crossing a stretch of desert at night. If the scenery in an area is particularly beautiful, however, take advantage of daylight driving so you can enjoy it!

Nighttime travel calls for you to be on the alert continually. It's easier to miss turnoffs and highway signs at night, especially in rural areas. Watch the gauges of your vehicle closely. Be alert for other drivers who may be handling their vehicles in an erratic manner.

41 🚗 Make Reservations

Roaming free and just following your whims can make for a wonderful adventure. Failing to do a little bit of planning in advance can also cause a trip to take a nosedive into disaster.

Have a Way to Get There—and Back If you are traveling by air during peak season, which is when most families travel, it's very important that you have round-trip reservations. Make your reservations far enough in advance to qualify for discounts—if you are able to do so—but also keep in mind that many discounted tickets are nonrefundable. If you think there's any possibility that you may not be able to take that cruise or make those flights, get a ticket that allows you some flexibility in rebooking. Notify an airline or cruise line as quickly as you realize that you aren't going to be able to use your reservation. (In the case of illness or death in the family, some nonrefundable tickets are partially refunded; in other cases, no refund is possible.)

Don't neglect to plan for ground transportation from airport, station, or port to your place of lodging. If you rent a car, you can save yourself some time at the airport by completing your reservations in advance. If you are relying on cabs, commuter trains, a subway system, or a resort-provided van or limo, get all the details well in advance of your departure.

Have a Place to Stay Again, make reservations as soon as you know how many of you will be staying for how long and what types of accommodation you desire. The best rooms and campsites are booked by those who know what they want, and if you're going to be paying full fare in peak season, you may as well find out which are the best rooms or campsites so you can request them!

Request no-smoking rooms if you want them, and ground-floor or second-story rooms if you want them. Ask about rooms with a scenic view. They may be well worth the extra dollars if you are going to be spending significant time in your room. If your room is only going to be a place to sleep, the view won't matter, and you may be able to save some money. Check on the accessibility between adjoining rooms (some join but only with a wall!), the availability of a roll-away bed or crib if you need one, and the approval for pets to stay (especially if you're taking one with you or you are highly allergic to a particular type of animal).

Even if you are following the road, wherever it may lead, you probably will have some idea around midday about where you are going to want to spend the night—at least to have a city of destination in mind. Call ahead to make sure there will be a room waiting for you. One family arrived in a major city thinking they'd have no difficulty booking a room upon arrival. They hadn't counted on three major organizations holding annual conventions in the city at the same time! They spent three hours frantically attempting to locate a room.

Major motel and hotel chains publish booklets listing all of their locations. You can request those you want in advance, usually at no cost, by calling a toll-free number. Take them with you if you are traveling by car, and again, take advantage of the toll-free numbers to make your reservations. If you have questions about the location of the hotel—for example, whether it's downtown in the business section or along the harbor (where you want to be) —ask for details. Once you have arrived in the city, you may want to call and get specific instructions on how to make your way to the hotel to save time and hassle trying to figure out which streets or exits to take.

Order Difficult-to-Get Tickets in Advance
Don't expect to arrive in New York City and find tickets to the most talked-about play available in all price ranges on a Saturday night in the summer! The same holds for any type of well-publicized or popular concert or event. Arrange for tickets in advance.

Make Reservations for Dinner
If you are planning on a formal dinner in a well-known restaurant or even if you want a meal in the resort

dining room where you are staying, make reservations. If you want to have dinner in a restaurant located in a major theme park, make your dinner reservations by 2:00 P.M. Reservations are especially important if you are planning to take in dinner before a performance of some type.

Remember the Confirmation Numbers
When making reservations of any type, you may be given a confirmation number. Keep track of this number until you have arrived and find your accommodations, reservations, or tickets in good order. (In the case of dinner reservations, you may want to request the name of the person who is taking your reservation.)

You may want to confirm your airline, cruise, or resort reservations a day or two in advance of your departure. It's worth the call to have the peace of mind in knowing that you are expected company.

Reservations are the key to avoiding disappointment. They still allow plenty of room for spontaneity.

42 🚗 A Devotional Time

Plan at least one spiritual event as you make your itinerary. It may be

- attending a religious service in a city you are visiting or participating in a nondenominational devotional time at the campground where you've parked your trailer.

- listening to a special series of sermons as you travel and having a time of family prayer at the close of the series.

- starting each day's drive with prayer and a psalm.

- spending a few quiet moments in a great cathedral, enjoying its beautiful stained glass windows or the music of the organ.

- attending a gospel songfest or getting tickets to a concert being performed by a Christian singer.

- seeing a passion play in a city along the way.

Just the Family You might want to create your own family devotional time some evening or on a weekend morning. You might even want to have such a time every day. Here are several suggestions:

Find a place of beauty Whenever possible, let nature inspire you and be your outdoor cathedral.

Assign a different role to each person One child might be responsible for reading a passage from the Bible, another for choosing the chorus that is going to be sung, yet another for closing or opening the family worship time in prayer.

Talk about spiritual matters You don't need to preach a sermon to your children—or they to you —but you can talk about the passage you've read or the songs you've sung, and share with one another what they mean to you personally. Don't hurry your time together. Give everyone an opportunity to say something meaningful.

Have a time of prayer Pray for your individual needs and your safety and health as you travel. Pray for protection over your vehicle and the travel of others. Pray for the people of the city that you are passing through—that they may come to hear the gospel and believe it. Pray for the pastors of the churches in the city, that they may be faithful ministers of the Word and loving servants to the people in their congregations. Pray for the loved ones you have left at home or you have visited on your trip. Pray for the safety of your home and neighborhood. Give praise to the Creator of the beauty you are experiencing.

Close your time with hugs and kisses all around
This is an excellent time to say "I love you" to another family member who may not have heard it in a while.

If you are outdoors and in a public place, you might find a way to make an offering as you enter or leave your chosen place of worship. Pick up any litter that you see and deposit it in a garbage bin. You'll be adding to the beauty of the place and making it even nicer for the next group.

You can spend ten minutes or an hour in such a family worship time. Don't be surprised if it's the part of your vacation that your children remember with great fondness in the years ahead.

43 🚗 A Watch for Each Person

Teach your child to tell time at an early age, and outfit her with a watch.

ETD and ETA Give your child estimated times of departure and arrival early in the day or the course of an event, and then update that information periodically. Let your child know when you leave your accommodations in the morning what you anticipate as your agenda for the day—where you are planning to go, about how long you anticipate staying in each place, and where you intend to be by nightfall.

Walk your child through the day mentally, and at the same time, give reference to the watch on his wrist. For example, "We're going to drive for an hour and then have breakfast. We'll probably be finished with breakfast by nine o'clock, and then we'll have about a two-hour drive to the beach. It should be about eleven o'clock when we arrive. We'll check into our room, unpack, and put on our suits. If you want, we'll take a swim before lunch. We'll spend the afternoon at the beach, at least until about four o'clock. Then we'll come back to the room, get showered and ready for dinner. After dinner, we may take in a game of miniature golf or see a movie, whichever you decide later that you'd rather do."

A watch and an overview agenda can go a long way toward eliminating the "when are we going to get there?" wail.

Keeping Track of the Time   If you allow an older child to make a foray into the mall or amusement park—or to go in a direction different from the one you want to take—set a meeting time and place, and synchronize your watches. Insist that your child show up on time (perhaps with a five-minute grace period). If she doesn't, curtail future roaming privileges. By the same rule, be on time yourself. No one needs to spend part of a family vacation waiting or worrying.

Ask your child to help you watch the time if you have parked in an area where you pay by the hour or have to feed a meter.

A watch also comes in handy in playing certain timed car games, in calculating miles per hour you are traveling, in determining where the turn-around point should be on the trail, and in making sure you don't overboil the eggs in the pot on the campfire.

If you are traveling across time zones, reset your watches to the new time. And remember to take them off before jumping in the pool!

44 🚗 A Child's Collection

Travel Memories   Help your child build an interesting collection that is related to your family travels. It may be

- a postcard album. Buy some cards to mail and some cards to keep. You'll probably want to note a date on each card and perhaps other information—such as who was along on the trip.

- a charm bracelet. Most major tourist attractions have some type of charm that can be added to a bracelet or necklace. Or you may be able to find generic charms upon returning home—perhaps a pair of skis or an ice skate to mark the winter holiday, or a tennis racket to remember times you played on the resort courts with family members or friends.

- shells or rocks. Again, label them as you gather them. But don't take anything that would be considered a violation of park or campsite regulations. All of the pieces of the

Petrified Forest should remain where they are!

- matchbook covers. Nearly every hotel, restaurant, and resort will have a personalized matchbook. If you have a young child, toss the matches (safely), and keep only the covers.

- stickers or hat pins. Decals, pins, and stickers are readily available as collectible items.

Or your child may want to collect something that will be useful later in life—perhaps miniature vases, suncatchers, potholders, demitasse spoons, or something of similar ilk.

The major point to remember is this: let the collection be one of your *child's* choosing. Your child will enjoy shopping along the way for just the right souvenir and will have hours of delight in looking at his finds while on the trip and back at home.

A Trip Scrapbook   If your child is a pack rat who enjoys picking up everything from brochures to wildflowers to matchbook covers to programs, suggest that she create a trip scrapbook upon her return home. In making such a scrapbook, your child is likely to be adding several more hours of fun to her summer.

45 🚗 A Personal Trip Diary

Encourage your child to keep track of personal impressions of your trip. Provide a little diary or a pad of paper for this purpose. Take plenty of pens and pencils (and a pencil sharpener) with you on your trip.

If your child is having a wonderful time, this is a great place for listing all the good times while the memory of them is strongest. If your child is having a terrible time, this is a great place for him to pour out his frustrations, anger, and negativity.

Your child's trip diary should be kept in confidence. Toward the trip's end, you might want to ask if she wants to read excerpts from her diary to the family.

Daily Entries Encourage your child to make daily entries—as you travel, during a break, in the quiet of the motel room at the day's end, after he's ready for dinner but still waiting on Mom and Dad.

Suggest that your child begin each entry with the date and the name of the place from which she is writing. Suggest that she tell what happened, describe things in detail, tell how she felt about certain events, and include an occasional funny anecdote, joke, or a blow-by-blow description of an amusing incident.

Laptop on the Road   If you have a laptop computer, you may want to take it along for some of the list, log, and diary activities suggested. Again, make sure that each person regards the privacy of all other diary or journal entries.

A Quiet Time for Reflection   Periodically choose to write in your trip diary—it might even be a poem. Your child will be more prone to keep a diary if he sees you keeping one.

Sketches, Too   Suggest that your child illustrate her private diary with sketches or crayon drawings. Point out to your child that what she writes will be a good accompaniment to any postcards or scrapbook materials she is collecting.

Do It for Grandma   If your child sees little purpose in keeping a trip diary, suggest that he write thoughts and memories for someone he loves so that he can give a more vivid description of the trip when he gets back home. Your child might also be more interested in keeping a trip journal if you point out to him that in doing so, he'll likely have his first homework assignment of the coming school year finished in advance. He will already have written the first draft of his "What I Did This Summer" essay!

46 🚗 Learn All You Can

Most national parks and major tourist attractions provide information centers and bookshops that present an outstanding array of historical and literary information. Find ways to incorporate these three layers of learning into your family vacation:

1. Learn all you can about a historical site or national park before you visit it.
2. Learn as much as you can while you're there.
3. If the place piques your interest, buy materials that you can read after you leave.

Don't be surprised if your child has a new interest in the history and literature of a particular time period after visiting a well-known landmark or building (such as Independence Hall and the Liberty Bell, Mount Rushmore, Stone Mountain, or Plymouth Rock) or after visiting a re-created historic village or restored neighborhood.

If you truly want to make your family vacation a learning experience, tie your trip in to what your child has just studied in school or what he is likely to be studying in the coming year.

Tourist Information Centers   Upon entering a new state, look for the tourist information center that's usually located close to the border. Take time to ask people who work there about the most scenic routes and the places you shouldn't miss. Pick up brochures about possible places to stay, things to do, or restaurants to try.

Historical Markers   Look for historical markers and signs along the way. Pull over and read them. It will take you only a few minutes to read the paragraph or two of information.

Local Color and Yarns   As you stop for an afternoon or midmorning snack in an area, try to find a local diner or mom-and-pop cafe. Ask the waiter to tell you the biggest news that's happened in recent years in the area where you are traveling. If you have noticed buildings of unusual design or have questions about certain items on the menu, ask about them. Perhaps the best information about a place is that picked up from people who live there. If you are traveling in a different region of the nation from the one you call home, your child will probably be fascinated by the different accents and vocabulary words. Strike up a conversation or two with the locals so your child can hear more and come to appreciate the cultural differences within her nation.

Remember, genuine spontaneous and activity-based learning is truly fun for a child.

47 🚗 Lots of Photos

Take lots of photographs. Don't skimp on film. Even if you get only three or four great shots from a roll, you'll be glad you have them later (and they might not have been the first ones you took in a place or of a particular person).

Close-Ups Are Desirable The panorama may be breathtaking. But chances are, your most interesting family vacation photos are going to be close-ups of people, animals, and activities. If you really want a beautiful shot of the big scene, look for a postcard, or pick up a color brochure.

Here are tips for making your family pictures more interesting:

Include people in the majority of your shots And rather than have a shot of one or more family members standing directly in front of the object being photographed, move the family members to the side, take a close-up of the family member with a tour guide in costume, or take a shot of the family member next to the sign that describes what you are seeing.

Look for unusual angles The head-on shot is usually the most obvious and most boring. Rather than take a shot of Dad standing in front of a giant redwood tree (and capture only the bottom twenty feet of the tree), try shooting up into the branches toward the sky or photographing the way a tree may be reflected in a puddle. If you want a shot of Dad in front of the tree, take a series of shots that you can roughly piece together to get a true sense of the height of the tree.

Rather than take a shot at the base of the Ferris wheel, try one from the top of it, looking down!

Choose the right film for the occasion If you want to capture action, purchase high-speed film.

Take time to get things in focus Nothing is more disappointing than finding that a photograph with a great expression and wonderful composition is out of focus.

Leave your flash at home Most of the photos that you want to take at night aren't going to turn out the way you envision they will. Using a flash attachment to capture an image more than twenty feet away is futile for the amateur.

Know Your Equipment
A family vacation is not the time to learn how to work a new video recorder or to become familiar with a new lens. Know how to use the equipment you're taking along and how to set up and shoot a photo in a matter of seconds.

Label Your Photos As soon as you have the photos developed, label them as to date, place, and names of people in the photo. (Your relatives fifty years from now will thank you.)

Get Double Prints Order double prints so your child can have her pick for a personal scrapbook or photo album.

Let Your Child Experiment Let your child take photos with his own camera. He'll learn a great deal through trial and error, and he'll have lots of fun along the way. He'll also be less adamant in expressing his desire to take photos with your camera.

Get Yourself in the Picture Don't let any person on the trip be the sole photographer. Such a person is rarely in any of the family photos.

48 🚗 Dress for Comfort

Travel Ease Dressing for comfort does not mean that you need to be sloppy or wear ill-fitting garments.

You need to feel good in what you are wearing Does the garment stretch when you do? Do you like the way the garment looks on you? Are you dressed appropriately for a wide range of activities and places?

Your travel garments need to require relatively little care Does the garment wrinkle easily or show stains readily? If so, you may start out the day feeling comfortable in it, but by the day's end, you'll be uncomfortable! Furthermore, you don't want to spend half of your vacation with an iron in your hand. Make sure that all garments you take on your trip are washable and that your child's wardrobe is stain resistant. Wash out difficult stains as quickly as you can.

The garments need to be right for the climate and activities of the place you are visiting The best travel outfits can be layered with shirts, sweaters, and jackets. You never know when the wind may shift, the fog may roll in, or the snow may start to fall. If you are taking a vacation to a winter resort —perhaps to go skiing—pack plenty of layers so that you can keep your skin dry. Take hand warmers and foot warmers if necessary, and don't forget your hat and gloves (as well as sunscreen and lotions).

Shorts are comfortable and fashionable, but if you are hiking long distances in rugged terrain or planning to have dinner in a major city, take along a pair of long pants.

Avoid garments that are overexposed. They rarely are in good taste and may keep you from being given entry into certain shops or restaurants.

You should take along shoes that fit A vacation isn't the time to break in new shoes. You will, however, need good support as you walk or hike your way through new places. A comfortable pair of walking shoes is hard to beat. Sandals are great for certain places, but they also leave feet exposed to sharp objects, pebbles, and thorns. Socks and sneakers are almost always a better alternative. If you are going to be in watery places where you are unsure of what lies on the creek or lake bottom, take along rubber or plastic shoes for each person to wear.

Your awake child should always wear shoes, except perhaps on rare occasions in the comfort of your car or van.

Take along a few extra sets of clothing That way if your child has an accident of some type, becomes ill, or inadvertently falls into the beautiful hotel fountain while reaching out to pet a goldfish, you will be prepared.

Knits and separates are great garments for a child on the go Choose printed fabrics (rather than plain colors). Velcro closures on your young child's shoes will keep you from stopping every few minutes to retie laces.

49 🚗 Invite a Friend to Go Along

A family vacation may be a lot more fun for all of you if you are able to invite a friend of your child to accompany you. This is especially beneficial if your child is an only child or there's a large gap between the ages of your children. Some families have found that the only way to get their teenagers and college-aged children to go on a family vacation is to make provisions for friends to go along.

A Trip Exchange You may be able to work out a vacation exchange with other families—their child or children go with you for a few days, and then at another time, your child or children go with them for a few days. That way, you, as parents, can enjoy a few vacation days alone together. Overall, the expense evens out. You'll probably need to invite a friend for each child in your family.

Insist that the visiting child become a part of your family instead of your child segregating himself with his friend and forming something of a subunit. The point of inviting a friend to go along is to enhance the fun for everyone, not to cause a division in family ranks. Include the friend in discussions, and give the friend a fair share of the trip responsibilities. Don't allow your child and his friend to gang up on other children in your family or shut them out of an experience.

Most important, make sure the friend who is invited to travel with you is someone that all members of your family agree to invite in advance and know fairly well.

Have an agreement with the other family in advance of your departure about what their child may and may not do, the limits of the discipline you may exact, and a general understanding of the amount of money their child should take along as personal spending money.

Family Caravans   Many families enjoy sharing vacations with other families—caravaning to a mutual destination, going on houseboats together, being a part of the same tour group, or camping together. You might consider this option if there is a family, or families, with whom you are close and have shared interests. Children in a caravan frequently trade riding positions for constant variety. Caravans tend to cover the miles more slowly than a single family. Once at a destination point, however, children seem to have multiplied fun in being able to play group games and to go as a group to planned activities while parents enjoy other entertainment. If a large enough group want to take a tour together, you may be able to qualify for certain travel discounts—a good option to consider if you'd like to go to an overseas destination.

A Baby-Sitter or Nanny You may find your family vacation more enjoyable for everyone if you can afford to take along your young child's regular baby-sitter or nanny. Don't expect the baby-sitter to work twenty-four hours a day. At the same time, neither you nor the baby-sitter should consider the trip as the baby-sitter's vacation. It's work! A baby-sitter can help you in a number of ways—with dressing and feeding children, watching children in the evenings while you go out to dinner, helping keep track of children in a crowded theme park, chaperoning part of your family should you need more than one motel room or suite. Make certain you have roles, responsibilities, and payment clearly spelled out in advance.

50 🚗 Shorter and More Often

The trend in family vacations is toward more frequent vacations of shorter duration. Don't overlook the value of a three-day or four-day weekend excursion with your family. It's a great option for going on winter retreats to the snow, for taking advantage of off-season travel packages, or for enjoying certain seasonal events, such as combining a fall foliage tour with an opportunity to pick up gifts and pumpkins in Lancaster County, Pennsylvania.

Consider This Some cruises now offer three- and four-day sails.

Many hotels offer reduced rates over weekends.

Air fares are frequently cheaper if you stay over Saturday night.

And employers are nearly always more flexible in allowing for a Friday or Monday away as opposed to your scheduling an entire week or two in one stretch.

Keep Your Focus The important thing to remember in a short family vacation is that you limit what you plan to see and do to two or three highlights. Consider, perhaps,

- a vacation to Kansas City in which you see a show at the Starlight outdoor theater in Swope Park, take in a Royals game, shop at Country Club Plaza and Crown Center, and have a steak or barbecue dinner at any number of fine restaurants.

- a long weekend in the high desert of California, taking in a round of golf in the morning with your teenager, a leisurely swim in the afternoon, and a game of tennis at night—with a long nap sandwiched in between.

- a before-Christmas trip to New York City to shop for presents by day and see a Broadway play at night. Your child will enjoy the opportunity to see the lights and displays along Fifth Avenue, skate in the rink at Rockefeller Center, and catch the view from the top of the Empire State Building or the World Trade Center. The trip out to the Statue of Liberty and Ellis Island is usually less crowded in winter months.

Each experience would be a weekend to remember—a distinct experience that serves as a mini-sampler to a particular city or region.

You may be able to afford such a trip once a year if you follow the next suggestion for another vacation time.

51 🚗 Stay in Town

One of the best options for a family vacation is to stay at home and play. This is an especially fun thing to do if both parents are working or children have been scattered in their activities for a several-month period.

A stay-at-home vacation is a good time to regroup as a family and get reacquainted with one another.

The important thing to remember is that you are all on vacation. Make this time distinct from other days at home. No lawn mowing. No cooking obligations for either parent. No running of errands or working at chores. Unplug the phone, and turn off the TV. Truly set aside the weekend or the days as a family event, and keep yourselves focused on one goal: having a good time together.

Swim   You may want to sleep in, then go out to breakfast. Find a local pool—perhaps at the "Y"—and pretend it's your own motel pool, or if you own a pool, take time to play in it and around it. Or you might want to spend a day at the local water park.

Relax   Spend a lazy hour or two with the paper. Stay in your pajamas all morning if you want. Watch a favorite video with your child, or introduce him to a video of the cartoons that were popular when you were his age.

Sightsee   Take in a tourist attraction or two—something you never think to do because it's right there in your hometown. It might be an art gallery or a museum, an aquarium or a zoo, or the tourist center at a major historical or cultural site.

Eat   Eat out, enjoy a picnic in one of your city's parks, or order take-out. Go to that new restaurant you've been wanting to try.

Beautify   If you have a teenage girl, you might want to plan some spa-style experiences to enjoy together—facials, manicures, pedicures, or experiments with new hairstyles. Or go to a salon and have those things done for you by a professional.

Go   Spend a couple of hours swinging a club at the driving range, riding the rides at the local amusement park, swinging a bat in the practice cages, taking a long bicycle ride along the riverfront trail, playing miniature golf, riding go-carts, or doing whatever it is that you or, better still, your child is always wishing you had more time to do together.

Drive up into the nearby foothills, go fishing, drive to the beach and get your feet wet in the surf, or drive out into the country to get some fresh air and see what's growing this time of year.

Schedule an evening outing at a theater or a concert. Plan in advance what you'd like to do if you were just visiting your city, and then choose to enjoy that activity together.

Maintain a Mind-Set   Going on vacation together is, to a great extent, a state of mind. You can choose to have that state of mind right in your home and save yourselves hours of packing, unpacking, driving, arranging for house sitters, pet sitters or kennels, yard and plant caretakers, as well as the expense of transportation and lodging. Your child and your spouse will no doubt enjoy the opportunity to play as a family, and many of the things that you would otherwise do on a trip you can also do as part of your at-home vacation, such as shopping for souvenirs and keeping lists and logs! Again, the number one rule is to have fun. Don't let yourself slide out of a vacation mind-set.

52 🚗 Let Your Child Tell About It

When the time comes to tell others about your family vacation, let your child take the lead. Ask her to give the highlights. You may be amazed at what she considers to have been memorable, fun, or unusual.

If you've taken video footage that now needs to be narrated, let your child add the music and the voice track. If you're making a scrapbook or photo album of your trip, write in it what your child says about each photo or item of memorabilia.

Relive Moments When something you saw, experienced, or did on your vacation appears as a setting or topic for a TV show (or news item), or when a family friend or relative brings up a topic that relates to your trip, ask your child, "Does that remind you of our trip? What do you remember most about our time there? Do you wish you were there right now?" While you're helping your child pick up his room, toss to him the stuffed fish that you picked up at the aquarium and say, "Aren't you glad this one didn't get away last summer?" The more you ask your child to recall your trip to-gether, the more your child will develop memories about the trip and come to value more highly the time you have spent together.

Periodically get out your photos or items that you collected from your trip, and take a look at them as a family.

Frame a favorite photo of your trip, and put it in your child's room. Let it serve as a reminder of a happy time and place with those who love your child the most: *you!*

As the Years Go By   Continue to let your child take the lead in telling about your vacation as the months and years roll by. The trip may change a little in its tenor or become exaggerated a tad in its "worst times" and "best times" narrative, but such is the ongoing life of a vacation! Family vacations can be a major factor in building family memories. Edit the facts related to a past journey if you must, but let the feelings flow freely. Above all, let your child have an opportunity to reflect upon the fact that you loved her enough to want to spend time with her, that you enjoyed your times together as a family, and that you took delight in introducing your child to a bigger world.

Your motivation for taking family vacations will eventually shine through. Make it a simple one: to show your child a good time as an expression of your love. Whether your trip is simple or extravagant, if your child comes away with that message, your time together will have been extremely valuable.